What Ha
E

MW00874655

A Cautionary Tale of
Failed Immigration Reform

By Jerry Kammer

Center for Immigration Studies
1629 K Street, NW, Suite 600
Washington, DC 20006
(202) 466-8185
center@cis.org
www.cis.org

ISBN-13: 978-1974356768

ISBN-10: 1974356760

About the Author

Jerry Kammer is a Senior Research Fellow at the Center for Immigration Studies. A former journalist, he received a 2006 Pulitzer Prize for helping uncover the bribery scandal centered on Rep. Randy "Duke" Cunningham. His work in Mexico for the Arizona Republic was honored with the Robert F. Kennedy Award for humanitarian journalism. Kammer holds a bachelor's degree from Notre Dame and a Masters in American Studies from the University of New Mexico. He also studied at Harvard on a Nieman journalism fellowship.

About the Center for Immigration Studies

The Center for Immigration Studies is an independent, non-partisan, non-profit, research organization. Since our founding in 1985, we have pursued a single mission – providing immigration policymakers, the academic community, news media, and concerned citizens with reliable information about the social, economic, environmental, security, and fiscal consequences of legal and illegal immigration into the United States.

The data collected by the Center during the past quarter-century has led many of our researchers to conclude that current, high levels of immigration are making it harder to achieve such important national objectives as better public schools, a cleaner environment, homeland security, and a living wage for every native-born and immigrant worker. These data may support criticism of U.S. immigration policies, but they do not justify ill feelings toward our immigrant community. In fact, many of us at the Center are animated by a "low-immigration, pro-immigrant" vision of an America that admits fewer immigrants but affords a warmer welcome for those who are admitted.

Table of Contents

Introduction

This book examines one of the most consequential failures in the recent history of American governance: the failure of the federal government to stop illegal immigration by enforcing the Immigration Reform and Control Act of 1986 (IRCA). That legislation, passed after five years of congressional debate, mandated civil and criminal sanctions against employers who knowingly hired unauthorized workers. This report also examines the related failure to fix the flawed system of worker identification that remains subject to the massive fraud that has foiled enforcement for more than 30 years.

As a result of those failures, IRCA has never come close to the goal that President Ronald Reagan identified when he signed it into law. Reagan said the legislation was intended to "establish a reasonable, fair, orderly, and secure system of immigration."[1] In a more precise formulation, a Department of Justice report in 1996 said the goal was "to reduce the magnet of jobs that draws illegal immigrants to this country and preserve those jobs for U.S. citizens and aliens authorized to work in the U.S."[2]

As this report will show, IRCA's failure had many causes: structural flaws written into the legislation; the political clout of business interests and immigration advocacy groups who resisted enforcement; the demoralization of federal immigration authorities who faced that resistance; and the ambivalence of public opinion that, while favoring limits on immigration, often recoiled from the human consequences of enforcing those limits.

As enforcement failed, the U.S. population of illegal immigrants grew from about 3.5 million in 1990 to its peak of 12.2 million in 2007. During that 17-year span, the unauthorized

1

population grew at an annual average of more than 500,000 persons, most of them drawn by the job magnet that IRCA was intended to deactivate. The influx validated a warning of the bipartisan Select Commission on Immigration and Refugee Policy. In its 1981 report to Congress, the commission recommended a sweeping legalization, but cautioned that unless legalization were combined with "strong, new efforts to curtail illegal migration" it "could serve as an inducement for further illegal immigration."[3]

IRCA's bipartisan congressional sponsors touted it as a compassionate yet pragmatic compromise that coupled a one-time amnesty for millions of illegal immigrants with an employer sanctions regime to ban the hiring of persons not authorized to work in the United States. Because the legislation also called for stepped-up border enforcement, it was often described as a "three-legged stool" of immigration reform.

Amnesty was granted to about 2.7 million people. But fraud immediately undermined the enforcement efforts of the Immigration and Naturalization Service (INS), a chronically beleaguered agency that was described in a 1986 congressional report as "undermanned, ill-equipped, and generally overwhelmed."[4]

Although IRCA required employers to verify that new hires were authorized, it provided no secure means to verify the authenticity of documents that workers presented for the Employment Eligibility Verification form, commonly known as Form I-9. Lawmakers, in an effort to accommodate new hires from a wide variety of backgrounds and social classes, allowed them to present documents issued by a wide variety of local, state, tribal, and federal agencies. Employers were legally obligated to accept a document that "reasonably appears on its face to be genuine."

The result, for many employers, was confusion and frustration. In a more general sense, the I-9 process created a moral hazard, a system of incentives that enables illegal immigrants to pretend to be legal while employers pretend to believe them. The 1-9 process became an administrative Potemkin village, an elaborate façade of legality. In 2006, David Martin, a former general counsel of the INS, wrote that fraud had reduced the I-9 process to "an empty ceremony". [5]

While IRCA's weakness was apparent from the beginning, most of the legislation's supporters did not anticipate that it would be exploited on such a massive scale. Many thought that the document fraud, which they had long confronted, would be contained within acceptable limits.

The INS, the executive branch agency within the Department of Justice that was charged with the responsibility for enforcing the law, launched an initially energetic "employer-labor relations" program to spread the word of employers' responsibilities. It also warned of civil and criminal penalties for those who knowingly hired unauthorized workers. The expectation, or at least the hope, was that the INS would bring employers into compliance with IRCA just as the Internal Revenue Service had long achieved taxpayer compliance with the tax code.

But the weakness of verification, the paucity of INS investigative resources, and tactical mistakes in levying fines on early violators, soon set worksite enforcement on a course to collapse. What followed was three decades of slow, steady enervation of enforcement. The exceptions were episodic exercises of political expedience when the administrations of Presidents Bill Clinton, George W. Bush, and Barack Obama conducted crackdowns in an effort to win public support for "comprehensive immigration reform" legislation that would once again combine legalization with promises of enforcement. The crackdowns, they thought, would ease public suspicion that Washington would walk away from enforcement once another legalization program was in place. That skepticism was the inevitable result of the collapse of IRCA's promise to demagnetize the worksite for illegal immigrants.

INS leaders bowed to pressure from Congress, including some elected officials whose early support for IRCA withered under pressure from employers who hired illegal immigrants. The INS eventually imposed restraints on the worksite raids that special agents conducted across the country to arrest illegal immigrants. Sometimes agents conducting raids acted so forcefully that they provoked public outrage, which then induced INS leaders to impose further restrictions. Agents in many INS district offices around the country saw funding "reprogrammed" away from worksite enforcement to less controversial work. Disgruntled special agents cited instances where colleagues had been detailed away from investigative work and assigned, for example, to work as an usher at a naturalization ceremony, or staff a public information desk,[6] or adjudicate petitions for naturalization.[7]

This report will examine the worksite enforcement strategies pursued first by the INS and then, following passage of the Homeland Security Act of 2002, by Immigration and Customs Enforcement (ICE). It spans the five presidencies that have been completed since President Reagan signed it into law and takes a brief look at the new Trump administration.

The most striking policy feature of the 31 years since IRCA became law has been the failure of successive administrations and congresses to reform the defective I-9 worker verification process, which was the legislation's critical birth defect. That deficiency remains, despite the efforts of many critics both within and outside the government. The most consistent critic has been the watchdog Government Accountability Office, whose many admonitions to Congress made it function like a Greek chorus in the protracted drama of IRCA's failure.

Efforts to reform the system intensified in the mid-1990s due to the work of the bipartisan U.S. Commission on Immigration Reform, which was chaired by former Democratic Rep. Barbara Jordan. The national mood at the time was influenced by rising anxiety about uncontrolled immigration. California was the bellwether in the backlash. Voters there in 1994 approved controversial Proposition 187, which sought to deny benefits to illegal immigrants. Susan Martin, the immigration scholar who served as the commission's executive director, recalled years later why she welcomed Jordan's appointment by President Clinton: "The situation had become so heated that I thought it would take someone with her gravitas and credibility to get past the emotion and bring people together with a reasonable solution," Martin said. "She was exactly the right person for that."[8]

The Jordan Commission, as it was widely known, urged Congress to mandate a computerized system that employers could access to verify work authorization. That recommendation met intense resistance from a strange-bedfellows coalition of ethnic advocates, libertarians of the left and right, free market enthusiasts, church groups, and business interests who had first come together during the 1980s debate that preceded IRCA.

Under intense pressure by the anti-enforcement lobby, Congress failed to fortify the worksite. Instead, it appropriated billions for the Border Patrol. That became a default policy position, a means to demonstrate toughness against illegal immigration. Public anxiety and frustration grew, stoking the 1992 and 1996 presidential campaigns of Patrick Buchanan, a fiery populist who vowed to stop the illegal influx.

Buchanan accused the federal government of abandoning American workers not only by failing to stop illegal immigration but also by facilitating the flight of manufacturing jobs to Mexico and other low-wage countries. In a book touted as "a nationalist manifesto", Buchanan recalled that when he visited American towns that corporations had abandoned "the story is always the same: bewildered workers wondering what happened to the good times, what happened to the town they grew up in, what's happening to their country" The book was titled *The Great Betrayal*.[9]

The anxieties of working-class Americans took dramatic shape in 2007, as President Bush called for passage of a package of reforms that became known as "comprehensive immigration reform" (CIR). In addition to repeating the IRCA formula of legalization-plus-worksite-enforcement, CIR proposed to allow low-wage employers access to hundreds of thousands of foreign workers every year. Public fury, stoked by conservative talk-radio programs, forced Congress to abandon that project.

That grassroots opposition asserted itself again to block House action on a comprehensive reform bill that the Senate passed in 2013. In 2016, that same populism was a propellant of the presidential candidacy of Donald Trump, who tapped public frustration and fury at IRCA's protracted failure. Trump's electoral success was due in part to IRCA's worksite failure.

This book is an examination of how and why that failure happened.

1. The Reagan-Bush Years

In October 1987, Alan Nelson, the commissioner of the Immigration and Naturalization Service (INS), called a press conference at INS headquarters in Washington. Flanked by senior staff on one side and statistical charts on the other, with an American flag behind him, Nelson stood at a podium and projected the confidence of an Army general in charge of a military campaign.

Nelson's purpose was to report on his agency's progress in implementing the Immigration Reform and Control Act, which had been passed nearly a year earlier. He pointed to a chart showing that the 1,124,931 arrests that the Border Patrol had recorded in the just-completed fiscal year represented a 30 percent drop from the year before. That, Nelson declared, demonstrated "that the immigration bill is beginning to work, that knowledge is out there, not only among American employers but potential illegal entrants."[10]

Turning to the agency's program to educate employers about their responsibilities under IRCA, Nelson said it was on track to complete a million informational visits by the following June. His personnel had also sent out seven million booklets that explained employers' obligation under the law to fill out a new document — dubbed Form I-9 — to verify that new employees were authorized to work in the United States.

"The law is beginning to work ... to discourage illegal immigration by turning off the magnet of jobs," Nelson said. He reported that employers were responding well to the INS effort to encourage their voluntary compliance. But he added the cautionary note that the six-month educational period provided by the law was over, so employers who failed to comply after receiving an initial warning from the INS were now subject to fines.

John Schroeder, the assistant commissioner for employer-labor relations, came to the podium to amplify Nelson's call for cooperation from employers, whose hiring practices IRCA was bringing under federal scrutiny for the first time. Schroeder had spent most of the previous year spreading the word around the country. In Dallas, for example, he spoke at an Hispanic Chamber of Commerce seminar titled "The New Immigration Reform Law and What Business Must Know and Do".

At the press conference, Schroeder praised the "good corporate citizenship" he had observed in visits with corporations like McDonald's, with its half-million employees, and Hyatt Hotels, with its workforce of 85,000. He said such relationships were "real good building blocks as far as the ability to show that it's not a difficult task to comply" with IRCA.

Business-Friendly Culture for IRCA Enforcement

In an interview in 2016, Schroeder recalled the business-friendly culture Nelson wanted to establish in the administration of IRCA. "His yardstick was not how many fines did we issue this month," Schroeder said. "It was how many people did we educate this month."[11]

Indeed, a few weeks before Nelson's press conference, the owner of Blackie's House of Beef, a popular restaurant in the nation's capital, had marveled at the change from days when INS agents chased his busboys and left him with a depleted crew. "Now they come to visit you and have you work with them," he told the *Washington Post*.[12]

Nelson's emphasis on the nice-cop strategy reflected the business-friendly politics of the Reagan administration. But at that 1987 press conference he also displayed the tough-cop credentials he had received from IRCA. Nelson announced that a Quality Inn in nearby Arlington, Va., just across the Potomac from Washington, DC, had become the first business to be fined under IRCA's employer sanctions provisions. He said the fine was necessary because the motel's managers had ignored an INS warning that they had hired unauthorized workers from Mexico, Guatemala, El Salvador, and Bolivia, "They just absolutely weren't complying in any respect," Nelson said. "And so we issued the fine."

Nelson's display of toughness on the East Coast was replicated by the INS district office in Los Angeles, home to the country's largest concentration of illegal immigrants. Employers began to adjust their business practices as word spread that the federal government was serious about enforcing the new law. Ten days after Nelson's press conference, the *Los Angeles Times* reported that hotel operators in Orange County were raising wages in anticipation of a tighter labor market. "Let's be realistic," said one business executive. "It just makes sense there will be greater competition for a smaller pool of employees."[13]

And so, when IRCA hit the one-year mark, it seemed to be working according to plan. The indications were that it was demagnetizing the American workplace. By tightening the labor market, it promised to make the law of supply and demand work on behalf of American workers rather than the employers who had relished the loose labor markets provided by illegal immigration.

Worksites Get Wise to the Myth of Enforcement

But it didn't take long for the myth of IRCA might to be knocked down. Seven months after Nelson's press conference, the *Los Angeles Times* examined hiring practices at hotels, car washes, janitorial services, landscaping companies, and construction firms. It concluded that IRCA's employer sanctions "simply aren't working." Most employers said they could not tell whether the documents workers submitted for the I-9 process — birth certificates, Social Security cards, green cards, and a host of others — were legitimate, the paper reported. "Many acknowledge that they knowingly accept questionable documents, while others are ignoring the law's requirements altogether."[14]

By 1989, the number of Border Patrol arrests dropped below one million for the first time in seven years. Skeptics suggested that was more an indication of the success of IRCA's amnesty than of its provisions for worksite enforcement. Those who had received amnesty no longer had to avoid the Border Patrol, they noted.

Meanwhile, immigration researchers at the University of California at San Diego reported that amnesty recipients were drawing unauthorized friends and relatives to join them by providing financing for the trip and assistance in finding work.[15] In 1990, the number of apprehensions jumped 23 percent to 1.2 million.[16] "The trend is not in the right direction," INS spokesman Duke Austin acknowledged.[17]

Also in 1990, two prominent immigration researchers warned that employers' initial belief that the federal government was serious about enforcing IRCA was "dissolving into complacency as employers experience the low probability of an actual

INS visit."[18] Those researchers, future INS Commissioner Doris Meissner and her future director of planning Robert Bach, would play pivotal roles in a controversial INS move to focus enforcement resources only on the most egregious violations of IRCA. With that decision, the INS effectively acceded to the illegality that became entrenched in U.S. worksites during the 1990s. We will examine the work of Meissner and Bach in the next section of this report.

In its failure to agree on a credible worker verification process, Congress, as we have seen, dropped IRCA into the lap of the INS with a crippling birth defect. That flaw was then compounded by the nice-cop culture that Congress and the Reagan administration had demanded. As some INS agents would ruefully put it, they were expected to act like Officer Happy.

This was bound to be a dicey proposition for INS special agents. Trained as criminal investigators, they had always had the job of arresting illegal immigrants and removing them from the country. But now, instead of just conducting searches or quick-strike worksite raids to arrest illegal immigrants, they were required to master the unfamiliar techniques of employer-labor relations. The potential for problems stirred anxiety at INS headquarters and at the Justice Department, which oversaw the agency.

"Suddenly you had a law enforcement workforce who were going to be interfacing with American citizens and businesses," said Anne Veysey, who was an analyst in the INS enforcement division. Veysey said there was alarm at the risk inherent in a situation involving agents accustomed to rounding up illegal aliens — as they were commonly known — who were not likely to complain. Under IRCA, those same agents were now investigating the hiring practices of American businesses whose executives often had friends in high places. "They were greatly fearful of that concept," Veysey said.[19]

And then there was the matter of self-interest at a government bureaucracy that, because of IRCA, would grow in budget and size. The INS did not want to establish a regulatory and enforcement regime so tough and punitive that it could antagonize business leaders and possibly lead to the repeal of employer sanctions. As one INS attorney put it, "If sanctions is sunset, we lose jobs and money."[20]

That anxiety took shape in an INS directive designed to regulate the regulators. Before agents could audit an employer's I-9 forms, they would have to notify employers three days in advance. "What that meant was that [during those three days] duplicate records were being created," Veysey said. The constraint aroused agents' suspicion that important people wanted to stifle worksite enforcement. "There was a constant battle with people who wouldn't allow us to actually take an enforcement posture," said Veysey.

The INS Investigations Division

IRCA created an enormous new set of responsibilities for the agents who worked under Jack Shaw, a former FBI agent who was the INS assistant commissioner for investigations. Their ranks, depleted by underfunding from Congress, had shrunk to about 900 nationwide when IRCA was passed. While Congress had authorized a near doubling of that force, the protracted congressional appropriations process led to hiring delays, which were followed by months of training before rookie agents were put to work.

The manpower shortage added to the difficulty of a task that some already thought was logistically impossible as well as politically unpopular. Even if the agents somehow reached Nelson's initial goal of visits to a million businesses, that would mean six million businesses went unattended in the vastness of the U.S. economy.

One of IRCA's principal congressional sponsors, Rep. Chuck Schumer (D-N.Y.), ridiculed the employer-labor relations initiative. Schumer mocked it as "this idiotic education program" and called for more robust enforcement. "No one expects you're going to have an INS agent in every factory all the time," he said, "But if employers know they're going to be enforced rather stiffly, they're going to obey the law."[21]

The most severe impediment to the work of INS investigators was the proliferation of the counterfeit documents trade. Counterfeiters had long been active on a relatively small scale. But after IRCA required employers to demand documentary proof of work authorization, the industry boomed. For less than $200, street-level salesmen could provide a suite of phony documents — Social Security cards, birth certificates, driver's licenses, visas — that made the holder appear to be authorized to live and work in the United States. Under the law, unless investigators found I-9 files whose documents were obviously fraudulent, employers could assert that they had acted in good faith and were therefore in compliance with the law.

A Jammed Enforcement Agenda, at the Worksite and Beyond

Even if INS special agents had received no new duties under IRCA, they would have had their hands full. In addition to pursuing illegal immigrants, they were expected to track hardened criminals and remove them from the country. They also had the jobs of investigating smuggling rings, money laundering schemes, and a category of crimes known as benefits fraud that involved efforts to obtain work authorization, green cards, naturalization, and other benefits. One common scheme involved bogus marriages between a citizen and a foreigner whose only true love interest was a green card.

Meanwhile, the growth of the INS investigations division was meager in comparison. The number of special agents did grow from 1,004 in 1987 to 1,625 at the end of the George H.W. Bush administration in 1993. But given the size and complexity of their responsibilities, they were badly understaffed. "We were given an impossible task," Jack Shaw said in 2017. "We did the best we could, but we couldn't really do anything more than present an illusion of enforcement. The resources just weren't there."[22]

Failure under the circumstances Shaw faced was probably inevitable. Shortly after IRCA was passed, the investigative workload grew dramatically because of a category of fraud triggered by a deal that Rep. Schumer cut to get the bill passed. To placate the politically powerful California growers, Schumer agreed to a provision for "special agricultural workers" who would be eligible for amnesty if they had worked 90 days in the fields. One of Schumer's negotiating partners in the deal was California Sen. Pete Wilson.

The SAW program demonstrated the congressional inclination to turn immigration policy into a piñata stuffed with visas for the benefit of influential constituencies. It triggered an avalanche of bogus applications for amnesty. Many of the applicants had never held a hoe in their lives, but they showed up at INS amnesty processing centers with proof of eligibility provided by the phony document industry. Labor contractors also got into the action. Some charged $1,000 for affidavits falsely attesting to the 90 days of work for former "employees".

The result, reported the *New York Times,* was "one of the most extensive immigration frauds ever perpetrated against the

United States Government."[23] The SAW program had been expected to accommodate about 350,000 migrants.[24] But more than 1.3 million applied and 1.1 million were approved.[25] Fraud was rampant, Shaw recalled in 2017. But because of political and institutional pressures as well as a shortage of INS agents, only a small fraction of those responsible for the fraud were prosecuted. Shaw summarized the instructions he received from his superiors this way: "You can't stop the process. You can't weed out who's legit and who's not legit. Get them through the system." He said the workforce demands of growers in California and Washington prevailed.[26]

The Border Patrol and Employer Sanctions

In an effort to distribute the worksite enforcement workload, the INS assigned Border Patrol agents to the employer education program. Many agents enjoyed the work. They found it to be an interesting change of pace from their usual duty of tracking illegal immigrants. "It meant you were in plain clothes and you weren't sweating in the desert," recalled retired agent Fernando Lucero, who worked in west Texas.[27]

Another retired Border Patrol agent, Mike Moon, said he had enthusiastically welcomed IRCA's attempt to shut off the job magnet. "I worked on the premise that if we started getting employers' attention, the word would get out," said Moon. "I thought that hiring people legally would become similar to paying your income tax."[28]

A similar optimism energized special agents of the INS Investigations Division. "There was a palpable excitement," recalled Dan Cadman, also retired." Naive as it sounds in retrospect, we felt on the cusp of great things."[29]

That can-do spirit soon began to fade. While some of the factors that undermined efforts to stop illegal immigration were written into IRCA, others were the result of administrative decisions. INS attorneys, seeking to avoid lengthy legal battles, routinely negotiated with businesses found to have violated IRCA. But instead of backing up agents' efforts to impose heavy fines, as the law provided, the attorneys frequently agreed to accept sharply reduced amounts that left investigators shaking their heads in demoralized disbelief.

INS agents suffered the morale-draining effects of seeing their investigative work result in fines so low that employers could shrug them off as a minor business expense. Bill Yates, a career INS official, recalled that "issuing fines that the attorneys mitigated down to nothing was not inspiring work."[30]

Mike Moon talked of one such case involving an El Paso Walmart that was charged with knowingly hiring five unauthorized Mexican workers to assemble bicycles. Moon called it a flagrant violation. "They were warned once and they did it again," said Moon, recalling that while the fine was originally assessed at $10,000, Walmart ended up paying about $3,000. "For a corporation as big as Walmart a fine like that is considered just more overhead, just part of the cost of doing business," Moon said. He added that the case was "a real morale killer" for agents in the field.

Morale had long been a problem at the INS. The agency's dysfunction had been laid bare in 1981 by a Pulitzer Prize-winning investigative series in the *New York Times*. The stories portrayed the agency as "a bureaucratic stepchild beset by political interference and official indifference, an agency mired in mountains of unsorted paper and hampered by lost and misplaced files, and with a record of selective enforcement, brutality and other wrongdoing."[31]

Alan Nelson, a former San Francisco attorney who had become commissioner in Reagan's second year as president, would resign under pressure in 1989, early in the term of President George H.W. Bush. He stepped down after an audit ordered by Attorney General Richard Thornburgh turned up evidence of continuing dysfunction. President Bush replaced him with Gene McNary, the Republican county executive of St. Louis County, Mo., where he had directed Bush's presidential campaign. McNary, like Nelson before him, came to the job with no background in immigration policy.

Frustrated Agents Look Away From the Worksite

Many special agents, disillusioned by what they saw as the politicization of worksite enforcement, gravitated toward investigative work that would not be stifled by the bureaucracy. Others became disillusioned with worksite enforcement because they found little satisfaction in arresting busboys or dishwashers.

During the 1980s, as immigration surged across the United States, law enforcement officials attempted to adapt to the growing involvement of non-citizens in drug trafficking, human smuggling, and related violent crimes that required sustained investigative work. Yates was assigned to the multi-agency Organized Crime Drug Enforcement Task Force, which sought INS expertise in prosecuting criminals for violation of immigration laws. This was a variation on the strategy that decades earlier had enabled federal agents to bust gangster Al Capone for tax evasion.

There were other opportunities for INS agents to take on hardened criminals. The Anti-Drug Abuse Act of 1988 expanded the INS role in the arrest and deportation of serious offenders.

In the early 1990s, Attorney General William Barr ordered the INS to assign agents to anti-gang enforcement efforts. Some agents would eventually take assignments with the Joint Terrorism Task Force, a nationwide partnership of law enforcement agencies.

Robert McGraw was one of the agents assigned to investigate drug trafficking by foreigners. In a 2017 interview, McGraw recalled that he encountered Jamaicans whose fathers had cut sugar cane in Florida but who themselves became members of violent trafficking gangs.

McGraw said he found such work more worthwhile and interesting than worksite enforcement, especially given the constraints imposed on employer sanctions work. "Cops are pretty practical people," McGraw said in an email. "Why go through the motions on worksite enforcement when we can enforce the law in such a manner that is truly important to the nation we cherish and swore to defend?"[32]

The IRCA mandate that employers accept documents that "reasonably appear to be genuine" resulted in legal battles over that standard's meaning for I-9 audits. In one instance, an appeals court overturned the administrative law judge's ruling that a Sizzler restaurant in Phoenix had knowingly hired an unauthorized Mexican immigrant named Armando Rodriguez. The INS attorneys argued that Sizzler employee Ricardo Soto should have been alerted to the fraud by the misspelling of Rodriguez's name on the Social Security card he presented. They also said the fraud would have been apparent if Soto had compared the card with the sample Social Security card in the employer's handbook the restaurant had received from the INS.

The court disagreed. "We can find nothing in the statute that requires such a comparison," it wrote. "Moreover, even if Soto had compared the card with the example, he still may not have been able to discern that the card was not genuine. The handbook contains but one example of a Social Security card, when numerous versions exist."[33]

That ruling highlighted another problem that made the I-9 process a source of torment and confusion for employers. The handbook presented them with 29 different documents that workers could present — including Social Security cards, immigration documents, birth certificates, and school records — some of which were produced in multiple formats. The General Accounting Office (whose name was changed in 2004 to the Government Accountability Office) would practically plead with the INS to trim the list of acceptable documents. But bureaucratic inertia stalled that effort, which was further complicated by the INS's effort to make the I-9 process user-friendly for persons — such as Native Americans on reservations — who might not have ready access to official documents. In 1999 the GAO reported that the agency "has made little progress toward its goal of reducing the number of documents that employers can accept to determine employment eligibility."[34]

The Paper Curtain

In 1991, the Urban Institute Press published *The Paper Curtain*, a book that compiled research on the worksite enforcement effort. Its title told the tale of the weakness of the employer sanctions effort. In a de facto rebuke of the INS, researchers cautioned that in order for enforcement to succeed it "must systematically reinforce the perception that the government attaches high priority to enforcing the law." They followed that general criticism with the specific admonition that "violations must be pursued aggressively — and lead to substantial fines and prosecutions."[35]

Researcher Michael Fix found problems that derived from the administrative decentralization that was entrenched in INS culture. The 34 district directors across the country had a remarkable amount of decision-making autonomy, Fix learned. The result, he said, was a nationwide patchwork of enforcement priorities. For example, in New York, Miami, and San Antonio, efforts to report drug dealers "dominated the enforcement agenda, and in Houston sanctions enforcement was almost entirely eclipsed by a local preoccupation with prosecuting fraud" by those who submitted bogus documents in an effort to prove they were eligible under IRCA's provisions for amnesty.[36]

The researchers found wide discrepancies in the fines levied against employers. Some districts preferred complex investigations that produced heavy fines for a few employers. Others focused on identifying paperwork violations associated with the I-9 forms that led to minor fines for many employers. "The INS does not need complete uniformity in the amount of the fines it levies, but there shouldn't be that sharp a variation," said Fix. "People have to be treated similarly place to place."[37]

The discrepancies highlighted another organizational problem at the INS, the free hand that district directors around the country were given to run their operations. As a result, wrote former INS general counsel Raymond Momboisse in 1989, the agency "functions as if it were composed of numerous totally independent units. ... and there has been no national uniformity in the enforcement of the law or implementation of policy."[38] Momboisse said the agency had become "totally decentralized and totally disorganized. There is a void of confidence, a feeling of drift, a loss of direction and motivation."[39]

In an effort to rationalize the work of the investigations division, the INS in 1991 issued a directive for a standardized use of investigative agents' time, with 30 percent to be used to investigate criminal aliens, 30 percent on fraud, and 30 percent on worksite enforcement.[40] Commissioner Gene McNary took employer education off the agents' to-do list.

The agents often worked in teams that focused on a particular enforcement area. The problem was that there were too many scams and too few agents. Supervisors in each area of enforcement — criminal aliens, smuggling, marriage fraud, and employer sanctions — competed for reinforcements. Meanwhile, Gregory Bednarz, a career INS agent who eventually became acting assistant commissioner for investigations, suffered through a yearly budgetary process in which requests for more enforcement resources — especially more agents — were routinely hacked to pieces as they ran the gauntlet of review at the INS, the Department of Justice, Office of Management and Budget, and congressional appropriators. "Very few of our requests for enhancements survived," said Bednarz in 2017.[41]

By 1990, the dysfunction at INS was only part of the explanation for the increasingly apparent failure of IRCA enforcement. The fundamental problem remained the same: the failure of Congress four years earlier to equip IRCA with a credible system of worker identification. Congress had bowed to the demands of the powerful left-right coalition that was led by business and ethnic groups, but also included church groups, immigration lawyers, business libertarians, and civil libertarians who warned that proposals for secure identifiers would foster a big-government assault against privacy rights. They also feared that IRCA would induce many employers to avoid hiring anyone who looked or sounded foreign.

In 1990, those same activist groups came together to demand that Congress repeal sanctions. Their warnings of discrimination had just received powerful confirmation in a report from the General Accounting Office, which found that IRCA had indeed caused "a widespread pattern" of discrimination.[42] That finding prompted a hearing before the Senate Judiciary Committee, where Massachusetts Democrat Edward Kennedy joined with Utah Republican Orrin Hatch in calling for a repeal of sanctions.

At that hearing, Mario Moreno of the Mexican American Legal Defense and Education Fund provided a poignant call for repeal as he asked for consideration of "the indignity, the pain, and the grim reality faced by minorities and foreign born workers" who were not being hired because of employer sanctions. He told the story of a Mexican-American job seeker who had been born in the United States but was turned away by an employer who demanded that he produce a document from the INS — which as a born citizen he never needed or received. "How much discrimination shall be tolerated by a nation committed to equal justice under the law?" Moreno asked. "We believe that the answer is none."[43]

That hearing featured tense exchanges between Kennedy's allies — MALDEF, the National Council of La Raza, the Conference of Catholic Bishops, and the American Bar Association — and the Senate's leading advocate of employer sanctions, Wyoming Republican Alan Simpson.

In a gesture that combined civility, irony, and exasperation, Simpson addressed these sometimes bitter antagonists as "the groups" or, ironically, as "old friends". In 1986, Simpson had reluctantly accepted severely compromised provisions for identification in order to win passage of a bill that would — at least and at last — outlaw the hiring of illegal immigrants. In 1990 Simpson ridiculed the notion that sanctions would be abolished. "We all know damn well it isn't going to be repealed," he said. "Go check with your friendly AFL-CIO and find out." In a reference to the president of the AFL-CIO, he said, "Thank heaven for Lane Kirkland."[44]

As the failure of enforcement became increasingly evident during the 1990s, the AFL-CIO would eventually reverse that position. As we will see, it would give up the fight against illegal immigrant workers and adopt a survival strategy based on recruiting them and pressuring Congress to grant them legal status.

The move to repeal sanctions fizzled in 1990, despite the efforts of the National Council of La Raza, whose president, Raul Yzaguirre, called it "the transcendent civil rights issue of our time."[45] Yzaguirre's organization was overtaking MALDEF as the most influential advocate of illegal immigrants. Cecilia Munoz, the NCLR's senior immigration policy analyst, wrote a paper that called on Congress not only to repeal sanctions but also to "reject proposals to develop any type of identity card" to improve the worker verification process.[46] The first page of her report described the NCLR as an organization whose mission was to "improve life opportunities for the more than 20 million Americans of Hispanic descent."

A Struggle Over Worker Verification

In late 1990, as Congress debated legislation to expand legal immigration, a dispute erupted between Hispanic representatives allied with the NCLR and Sen. Simpson, who had long claimed to be pursuing immigration policy in the broad national interest.

The dispute concerned Simpson's attempt to insert a provision for a pilot project to develop a secure driver's license that would include a biometric component, perhaps a fingerprint, and the driver's Social Security number. His hope was to develop a form of identification that would eventually be used to stop illegal immigration at the worksite.

Simpson's effort was blocked by a group of Hispanic members of Congress who were led by Rep. Ed Roybal of California. During floor debate, Roybal associated Simpson's effort with a particularly sinister form of racism. "It is ironic that South Africa has just abandoned its notorious pass-card identification program that has been an essential element of its hated apartheid system," he said. Such overwrought language, reflective of emotions that were rooted in the discrimination Roybal had experienced as a young man in East Los Angeles, was common in the debate over proposals for more secure worker identification. For civil libertarians and free market conservatives, calls for more efficient identification stirred anxieties of Big Brother totalitarianism.

The Problem of Criminal Aliens

That 1990 Senate hearing on employer sanctions foreshadowed a problem that would spread across the country in the 1990s. During that decade, as the nation's illegal immigrant population surged, the INS increasingly focused its enforcement attention on those whose violations of law went beyond immigration infractions. Because they were seen as an immediate threat to public safety, they became a prime concern of congressional appropriators who controlled the INS budget.

At the hearing, Sen. Paul Simon (D-Ill.) asked Gene McNary about the case of Jose Ramon Orantes Pleitez, an illegal immigrant who had been arrested in New York, then released pending a deportation hearing, for which he failed to appear. Orantes Pleitez fled to Illinois, where he was detained by police for trespassing at an Air Force base. Police brought his illegal status to the attention of the INS, which declined to take him

24

into custody because he had not been convicted of a crime. He then stole a pickup truck that he crashed into two pedestrians, killing them both.[47]

"He's an illegal alien, and at the present time that is not a priority situation for our law enforcement people," said McNary. Jack Shaw joined in with a statement about INS priorities in the face of an overwhelming workload. "Our focus today is on criminal aliens," said Shaw, adding that the INS was receiving about 100,000 calls annually from law enforcement agencies across the country that had detained illegal immigrants. But unless they had been convicted of a crime, they were not a priority for Shaw's agents. Over the next 15 years, Congress would repeatedly appropriate funds to provide the INS with more detention space to hold criminal aliens whose proliferation, in large measure, was the result of the failure of worksite enforcement.

2. The Clinton Years

Bill Clinton became aware of the political dangers of chaotic immigration long before he became president. In 1980, when Clinton was governor of Arkansas, he lost reelection to a challenger whose TV ads portrayed him as weak in his response to rioting Cuban refugees at Fort Chaffee, Ark., where they were being held for screening. The turbulence intensified anxiety among those who thought the United States was under siege and the government was complicit in the foreign intrusion. Years later, the *Washington Post* reported on that episode under the headline "The forgotten story of how refugees almost ended Bill Clinton's career".[48]

In 1993, during Clinton's first months in the White House, a series of incidents seized the nation's attention and aggravated its immigration angst:

- Zoe Baird, Clinton's choice to be attorney general, withdrew her name from consideration, conceding to the fury that followed revelations that she had hired two illegal immigrants from Peru as a nanny and chauffeur, and then failed to pay Social Security taxes.

- A Pakistani who had applied for asylum in the United States killed two CIA employees in a shooting rampage outside the agency's headquarters in suburban Washington. CBS reporter Leslie Stahl reported on "60 Minutes" about rampant abuse of the asylum system by foreigners who appeared at Kennedy Airport with phony documents. They were admitted into the country and received permits to work until their asylum hearings, for which few appeared. "It's so easy to defeat the system," an INS official told the *New York*

Times. Another official added, "The aliens have taken control. The third world has packed its bags and it's moving."[49]

- A Kuwaiti who had entered the United States with fraudulent documents and asked for asylum blew up a yellow Ryder rental van filled with explosives in the garage below the North Tower of the World Trade Center.

- The *Golden Venture*, a dilapidated cargo ship smuggling several hundred Chinese ran aground off New York. Ten people drowned or died of hypothermia in their attempt to reach shore. The story of that tragic odyssey alerted Americans to the brutal world of the "snakeheads", smugglers who were funneling tens of thousands of Chinese into the United States at a per capita cost of $30,000 or more.

The drumbeat of stories warned of disorder, danger, and lawlessness in an immigration system that was under-regulated and overwhelmed. Public concerns intensified when the nightly television news showed thousands of Haitian and Cuban "boat people" approaching the Florida coast, hunger and desperation etched in their faces.

The Clinton years, 1993 to 2001, were a decisive time in the story of illegal immigration. At first, INS enforcement expanded in response to public outcry and Clinton's determination to avoid another Fort Chaffee-style political debacle. Then it imploded under an array of economic, political, demographic, and social pressures. This allowed an immense and protracted burst of illegal immigration from Mexico. Word spread that U.S, employers' interest in Mexican labor was strong, worksite enforcement was weak, and it was easy to get lost in the interior of the United States.

Late in the decade, as the U.S. economy boomed and the unemployment rate dropped to 4 percent, Richard Stana of the GAO sized up the state of worksite enforcement at a congressional hearing. Stana said most illegal immigrants "are well aware that the enforcement mechanism is modest and that they stand a good chance, once across the border, to find employment."[50] the *Washington Post* reported that flimsy enforcement combined with the easy availability of fraudulent documents to create a "pull factor that encourages people to risk crossing the border illegally ... or to use various other means to gain entry."[51] IRCA enforcement went bust long before the economy's dot-com bubble collapsed at the end of the decade. Far from shrinking illegal immigration, IRCA had encouraged it. Instead of deactivating the jobs magnet, IRCA had supercharged it.

In 1994, President Clinton recognized the political danger in the populist backlash against illegal immigration. Nowhere was the climate more tense than in California, where Republican Governor Pete Wilson was blaming Washington for the chaotic influx that played out in plain view every night just south of San Diego. Initially far behind in the polls, Wilson rode Proposition 187, the anti-illegal immigration ballot measure that was passed with 59 percent of the vote, to an easy reelection victory.

Clinton, wary of both the backlash and a potential challenge from Wilson in the presidential election of 1996, ordered Attorney General Janet Reno to California. There she directed a buildup of the Border Patrol, which launched Operation Gatekeeper in an attempt to impose order on the borderlands chaos. Border fencing, cameras, and lighting were part of the effort as Reno vowed that the Clinton administration would deliver "a secure border that is fully defensible against illegal immigrants."[52] She then added a steely-eyed pledge: "We will not rest until the flow of illegal aliens has abated." Such never-retreat declarations from officials in the Clinton administration became a regular feature of 1990s immigration reporting.

To understand the Clinton administration's failure to fulfill that pledge, it is useful to look at an assessment that respected demographer Jeffrey Passel would make seven years after Clinton left office. Writing for the Pew Hispanic Center, Passel observed, "The spread of immigration flows to new areas (largely driven by new settlement patterns of unauthorized Mexican immigrants) has transformed the political issue of immigration from a largely local concern (in six states) in the early 1980s to a national issue now."[53]

But in 1994, Clinton was focused on short-term political danger. Operation Gatekeeper calmed the chaotic corridor that stretched north from Tijuana, thereby easing Clinton's political problem. However, it didn't close the gate. It merely shifted it to remote stretches of the border. Smugglers, so wily and tough that Mexican slang named them "coyotes", adjusted their routes and raised their prices.

INS criminal investigators were surprised by the intensity of the counterfeit-documents trade that served illegal immigrants once they reached their destination. "There's so much money associated with it that every time we arrest and prosecute a ring, there's always somebody to step in behind them," said John Brechtel, who supervised INS investigations in Los Angeles.[54] When agents in Los Angeles busted a counterfeiting ring, they seized 115,000 blank documents — including green cards and Social Security cards — with an estimated street value of $5 million.[55]

Despite such arrests, the phony-document trade was so lucrative that other groups rushed in to meet the demand from illegal immigrants. Labor economist and immigration expert Philip Martin reported that, despite Operation Gatekeeper, many illegal border-crossers made it past the Border Patrol on their first attempt. In the understated tone of someone drawing attention to an obvious problem that has long been overlooked, Martin said, "Many believe that the INS should devote more resources to interior enforcement to prevent unauthorized workers from obtaining U.S. jobs."[56]

Barbara Jordan and the Commission on Immigration Reform

As Janet Reno was pouring federal resources into the border, the U.S. Commission on Immigration Reform, under the leadership of civil rights icon and former Democratic Rep. Barbara Jordan, presented a proposal to repair the hole that counterfeit documents had punched into worksite enforcement. The commission called for pilot programs to test systems for a computerized registry of information supplied by the INS and the Social Security Administration. Employers would be able to access the registry by telephone to learn if Social Security numbers presented by new hires were valid and had been issued to someone authorized to work. While the commission acknowledged that there could be challenges to such a system, its 1994 report to Congress asserted that the pilot programs would provide "an opportunity to determine the most cost-effective, fraud-resistant, and non-discriminatory method available." That report, titled "U.S. Immigration Policy: Restoring Credibility",[57] became the basis for legislation sponsored by Republicans Alan Simpson in the Senate and Lamar Smith in the House.

The commission's report and the legislation it inspired drew fierce opposition from the left-right coalition that had long resisted immigration enforcement. Lucas Guttentag of the

ACLU warned that the proposals to reform worker verification were "merely a launching pad for a national computer registry and a de facto ID card system that will make human guinea pigs of millions of people in the states where the system is supposed to be tested." The National Rifle Association joined in, sounding an alarm about government intrusion into personal privacy. Cecilia Munoz of the National Council of La Raza, fearing that employers would only check the status of minorities, denounced Jordan's proposal as "worse than Big Brotherism" for Latinos.[58] Republican insider, free market advocate, and Microsoft lobbyist Grover Norquist orchestrated a protest that likened the proposal to Nazi dehumanization of Jews: "We had guys walking around with tattoos on their arms," he said. Stephen Moore of the libertarian Cato Institute added another note of Manichean struggle. He said Jordan had made "an evil proposal. ... the camel's nose under the tent for a national ID card." [59]

Conflicting political considerations put the Clinton White House on a zigzag course. While Clinton was attuned to growing public anxiety about illegal immigration, he had political allies and donors who wanted expansive immigration policies and compassion for illegal immigrants. Meanwhile, economic and demographic forces were intruding from south of the border. In Mexico, an economic crisis in 1995 wiped out a million jobs, even as the Mexican working-age population was exploding in a baby boom that between 1970 and 2000 would swell the population from 53 million to 100 million.[60] The result was an exodus to the United States, much of it illegal and much of it to Arizona, where schools, hospitals, and social service agencies experienced tremendous new demands for their services.

In his 1995 State of the Union address, Clinton talked tough about illegal immigration. "All Americans, not only in the states most heavily affected but in every place in this country, are rightly disturbed by the large numbers of illegal aliens entering our country," he said. "The jobs they hold might otherwise be held by citizens or legal immigrants. The public services they use impose burdens on our taxpayers." Clinton pledged "to better identify illegal aliens in the workplace as recommended by the commission headed by former Congresswoman Barbara Jordan."

Clinton introduced a theme repeatedly raised by Jordan. "We are a nation of immigrants, but we are also a nation of laws," he said. "It is wrong and ultimately self-defeating for a nation of immigrants to permit the kind of abuse of our immigration laws we have seen in recent years, and we must do more to stop it." Jordan issued a blunt warning that failure to manage immigration would provoke an anti-immigration backlash. "Unless this country does a better job in curbing illegal immigration, we risk irreparably undermining our commitment to legal immigration," she said.[61] The possibility of a populist backlash against unchecked immigration was given ominous form by Sen. Dianne Feinstein (D-Calif.): "Ladies and gentlemen, let me say to you what I honest-to-God believe the truth. If we cannot effect sound, just and moderate controls, the people of America will rise to stop all immigration."[62]

Clinton's initial endorsement of Jordan's recommendations aligned him with a formidable and beloved national figure whose stature he had acknowledged in 1994 when he awarded her the Presidential Medal of Freedom. Jordan was "the most outspoken moral voice of the American political system," Clinton said. He also said Jordan had "captured the nation's attention and awakened its conscience in defense of the Constitution, the American dream, and the community we share as American citizens." Elaine Jones, director of the NAACP Legal Defense Fund, added this: "Barbara understood that the law was the fabric of society."[63]

33

Rhetoric Meets Reality, and Loses

Clinton's soaring rhetoric clashed with the brutal reality of the American workplace, where many business leaders were delighted with the availability of low-wage unauthorized workers. The attractiveness of unauthorized workers to unscrupulous employers was famously described by Ray Marshall, President Carter's liberal secretary of labor, who observed that they worked "hard and scared".

During the 1990s, many states that had experienced little immigration for decades — including Georgia, North Carolina, and Iowa — saw rapid growth in their immigrant populations. While estimates at the time put the annual growth of the unauthorized population at about 250,000, demographers would later double that estimate as they got a clearer picture of the dimensions of the influx. The Pew Research Center would report that between 1990 and 2000 the nation's illegal immigrant population grew from 3.5 million to 8.6 million. So the average annual increase exceeded 500,000.[64]

California continued to attract the largest numbers of newcomers, both legal and illegal. But even there the INS Investigations division, which had the job of enforcing employer sanctions, remained a 98-pound weakling. In 1995 the *Los Angeles Times* took the measure of the mismatch, reporting that in Southern California "only 30 to 35 INS agents monitor almost half a million employers in a vast area stretching from San Clemente to San Luis Obispo, and east to the Nevada and Arizona borders." Jack Shaw, who directed the INS investigations division, said, "Sanctions have not been supported with resources. If we're not visible, no one takes the law seriously."[65]

The 1995 Crackdown:
Operation SouthPAW and Worksite Raids

Lee Bargerhuff, the agent in charge of the Border Patrol's San Antonio station, received an abrupt lesson on the politics of enforcement policy in 1995 when a secretary interrupted his briefing of special agents who were about to conduct a worksite raid at a Luby's cafeteria. U.S. Rep. Henry Bonilla, who represented the city, was on the phone. A year earlier Bonilla, a Republican, had called for a crackdown on illegal immigration. But this time he had a different message. Somehow he had found out about the impending raid. He wanted Bargerhuff to go easy on Luby's, whose corporate headquarters were in San Antonio. Constituent service trumped worksite enforcement.

"The congressman told me Luby's was an important corporate citizen, and he said that surely we could work something out," Bargerhuff recalled in 2017.[66] Bargerhoff replied to the congressman that if Luby's had been willing to address INS concerns about its hiring practices, there would be no need for a raid. "As politely as I could, I told him my orders didn't come from him and that he wasn't in my chain of command," Bargerhuff recalled. He said he then resumed the briefing, only to be interrupted again, this time by a blunt message from the headquarters of the Laredo sector. "They told me the operation was scrubbed," he said.

At the INS office in Atlanta, district director Tom Fischer received a stream of calls in 1995 from people who were alarmed at the crowding of schools and neighborhoods resulting from the big migrant influx. "They were asking me, 'What the hell are you guys doing and why don't you do something about this?'" Fischer later recalled. [67]

Meanwhile, an INS colleague in Arkansas, where the poultry industry was matching the public's growing appetite for poultry with its own appetite for immigrant labor, wrote a memorandum that assessed the situation there. "The large number of illegal aliens and our inability to deal with them has brought criticism and the notion that we have become an inept agency unable to enforce our immigration laws in the interior of the United States," the internal memo said. It called for action "to change this negative perception, enhance our image and regain the confidence of our citizens."[68]

Those concerns generated an enforcement campaign that took its name from an admonition Fischer had received from his wife's aunt. "She asked me, 'Why aren't you protecting American workers?'" Fischer said. Condensing those last three words to their initials, he introduced Operation SouthPAW, a new attempt to deliver on IRCA's old promise.

SouthPAW mobilized dozens of INS agents to pursue tips that came primarily from authorized workers and the public. They conducted raids at construction sites, carpet factories, hotels, poultry plants, and other worksites in Georgia, Alabama, Arkansas, Tennessee, and the Carolinas. They arrested 4,044 unauthorized workers, about 90 percent of whom were from Mexico. The rest were from 40 other countries in Latin America, Asia, Eastern Europe, Africa, and the Middle East. In a pamphlet titled "Worksite Enforcement: Reducing the Job Magnet", the INS boasted that because of their removal $55.7 million in wages were made available to American workers.[69] Adding a new twist to the old tactic of worksite raids, Fischer worked with employment agencies to fill suddenly vacant jobs with authorized workers. He touted the results in regular statements to the press. "We're going to ensure that the American worker is protected," Fischer said as he supervised a 1996 raid at a carpet factory in Dalton, Ga.[70]

SouthPAW triggered alarms at the National Immigration Forum, a Washington-based advocacy group that tied together the left-right coalition for expansive immigration. "It smacks of a kind of police approach," said Frank Sharry, the forum's executive director, who wanted the INS to back off. *USA Today* observed that "immigration advocates, many of whom have supported Clinton, are growing increasingly bitter, convinced he's been influenced by public resentment of illegal immigrants."[71] While that argument would gain political power as both legal and illegal immigration continued to grow, Tom Fischer received so much support that top-level INS officials who wanted to rein in the raids kept quiet. "They really couldn't shut us down because the public reaction was so good," said Fischer.[72] For Clinton, who was as attuned to public unrest over illegal immigration as he was fixated on his campaign for re-election, it was a bad time to accede to the wishes of Frank Sharry and his allies.

The 1996 Battle in Congress

The 1994 mid-term elections put Republicans in control of the House and Senate for the first time in 40 years, enabling two Republicans, Sen. Alan Simpson of Wyoming and Rep. Lamar Smith of Texas, to become chairmen of the immigration subcommittees in their respective chambers. Because the national mood had grown stern about illegal immigration, they were confident of winning enactment of the Jordan commission's proposals for stopping illegal immigration and redesigning legal immigration.

Testifying at a Senate hearing before the election, Jordan issued a call to action: "It is both a right and a responsibility of a democratic society to manage immigration so that it serves the national interest," she said. Later she declared that the commission found that there was "no national interest in continuing to import lesser-skilled and unskilled workers to compete in the most vulnerable parts of our labor force. Many American workers do not have adequate job prospects. We should make their task easier to find employment, not harder."[73]

Simpson and Smith had hoped to win mandates for a robust and mandatory system to verify workers' legal status. They failed. Their effort to boost worksite enforcement was cut down to a pilot project in a few states where employer participation would be voluntary. The two lawmakers also adopted the Jordan commission's recommendations to redesign legal immigration policy to prioritize the speedy reunification of nuclear families while curtailing the "chain immigration" system. That system allowed a single immigrant gradually to bring an extended family to the United States, including siblings, cousins, parents, and grandparents.

The reform proposals for legal immigration also drew intense resistance. President Clinton backed off his endorsement of Jordan's proposal, bowing to opposition that included organizations of Asian-Americans who wanted to protect the chain immigration. Karen Narasaki of the National Asian Pacific-American Legal Consortium denounced the commission's recommendations as "an attack on the Asian community."[74] Silicon Valley entrepreneurs joined in to protect their access to skilled foreign workers. The effort to reform legal immigration policy was routed by its well-organized and influential opponents.

A Split Between Democrats

While most members of the Democratic coalition opposed Simpson and Smith, some held to the traditional Democratic concern for working-class Americans. That concern had launched the long debate that culminated in the 1986 passage of IRCA. But as illegal immigration became entrenched and Hispanic political power grew, many Democrats abandoned the old liberal efforts to stop illegal immigration. Latino activists had become an important part of the Democratic coalition.

A 1996 debate on the floor of the House of Representatives included a vivid exchange between two of the most liberal Democrats that put the party's divide in sharp relief. John Conyers of Michigan invoked the civil libertarian argument about the dangers of government regulation: "This is the famous camel's nose under the tent amendment," Conyers warned indignantly. "This is the one where it starts off real nice. Not to worry, folks. It is okay. Trust us. ... We will do it just like we did the Japanese internment program when we said we are going to find out who the Japanese are that need to be rounded up."[75] Like many other Democrats, Conyers was a crusader for social justice who came to see efforts to stop illegal immigration as a social injustice.

The response from Rep. Barney Frank of Massachusetts blended incredulity with sarcasm about the internment camp analogy. "We are not talking about camels, noses and tents," Frank said. "We are talking about whether or not we have a rational approach to enforcing the laws against illegal immigration. I have to say that, of all the things in my life that puzzle me, why so many of my liberal friends have such an aversion to this simple measure is the greatest. ... To turn this into some act of oppression makes no sense whatsoever."[76]

Alan Simpson was accustomed to accusations of big-government oppression from the left-right coalition that had fought immigration enforcement for decades. In 1996, he was also infuriated by what he saw as cynical machinations at the Immigration and Naturalization Service. At issue was a blatantly misleading INS press release that suggested there was no need for such legislative action because immigration was slowing on its own, due to a reduced demand for green cards. Questioning Commissioner Doris Meissner at a Senate oversight hearing where she was the only witness, Sens. Simpson and Feinstein accused the INS of politically motivated deception to derail the proposal to reduce legal immigration.

"What [the press release] created was a real distortion in what we were trying to do and made it falsely look like we were reducing the numbers, when in fact the numbers were increasing dramatically," said Feinstein. "I think it created, for me at least, a major credibility problem ... because this was hotly contested" in the Judiciary Committee. Simpson, declaring his respect for Meissner, said he did not blame her for the press release. But he cautioned her that she had been "ill-served" by others at the INS, people who "have simply political interests at heart, and that does not serve the country's interest well."[77] He did not name names.

No Lobby for American Workers

The Jordan commission's work represented a high-water mark of efforts to stop illegal immigration and to reduce legal immigration. When Jordan died in early 1996, at the age of 59, those efforts lost their most powerful voice, the voice least likely to be silenced by accusations of guilt by association with bigots or Big Brother. In a tribute to Jordan, Simpson said, "If she had been here, we would have gotten a lot further."[78]

In 1997, Robert Reich, who had been labor secretary during President Clinton's first term, lamented the absence of a Washington lobby that could challenge the tenacious and well-funded coalition that hacked away at the efforts to enact measures for effective worker verification. "There's no National Association of Working Poor," said Reich. "There's no special-interest lobbying group working on behalf of very poor people trying desperately to find and keep jobs.[79]

Susan Martin, who had worked at Barbara Jordan's side, was part of a team of Georgetown University researchers who in 2007 issued a blunt assessment of protracted congressional failure to enforce immigration law within the United States. They reported: "Despite acknowledgment of IRCA's ineffectiveness in stemming illegal immigration by analysts from a multiplicity of political perspectives, disciplines, and institutions cross-cutting the academic, government, labor, and advocacy communities, there has been little political will for worksite enforcement since its passage in 1986. In its place, Congress has primarily channeled resources towards securing the southern border."[80]

The John Huang Connection

An investigative report by the *Boston Globe* detailed a campaign by Asian Americans to persuade President Clinton to reverse his early endorsement of Jordan's proposal to end chain migration. The *Globe* reported that the reversal "brought the White House in line with the top priority" of Asian-Americans who had contributed heavily to his campaign.[81]

The *Globe* conducted a follow-the-money investigation of the advocacy of John Huang, an immigrant from Taiwan who in 1992 had raised $250,000 for Clinton's first presidential campaign.[82] Four years later, he was credited with raising about $3 million for Clinton's re-election. By then he was a vice chairman of the Democratic National Committee. The *Globe* reported that Huang "waged an intensive effort to influence Clinton's migration policy."

In a remarkable coincidence, Huang had earlier been appointed to a policymaking position at the Commerce Department for which he was "totally unqualified" according to the congressional testimony of a former undersecretary for international trade.[83] Huang worked under Charles Meissner, the secretary of international economic policy and the husband of INS commissioner Doris Meissner. Charles Meissner died in the 1996 plane crash in Croatia that took the lives of Commerce Secretary Ron Brown and others. In 1999, Huang pleaded guilty to a felony conspiracy charge for violating campaign finance law. His story is an example of the links between campaign fundraising and public policy in Washington.

Tough Talk on Deportations

Just before the 1996 election, the White House held a press briefing to boast about record numbers of deportations of illegal immigrants. "I am proud once again to announce that the Clinton administration's determination to remove criminal aliens and other deportable aliens from the United States has produced record results," Meissner announced.[84]

Meissner said 67,094 illegal immigrants — criminal and non-criminal — had been deported in the 1995 fiscal year. In a dutiful tribute to Clinton that echoed statements from the White House and the Justice Department, Meissner contrasted his performance to that of his predecessors. "For too many years, under-enforcement of our nation's immigration laws undermined their credibility," she said. "But this administration's unprecedented expansion of and support for strong but fair enforcement of immigration laws ... is restoring that credibility."

In another bow to Clinton's leadership, Meissner declared that the INS "means business when it comes to enforcing immigration laws in the workplace." That echoed language Clinton had used the day after Pat Buchanan's surprising second-place finish in the Iowa caucuses, when he issued an executive order barring companies that had knowingly hired unauthorized workers from receiving government contracts. "American jobs belong to America's legal workers," Clinton said. "This executive order will make clear that when it comes to enforcing our nation's immigration laws, we mean business. We are determined to restore the rule of law to our nation's immigration system."[85]

Despite the stern rhetoric from the president and the INS commissioner, the illegal immigrant population continued to surge as the business of evading IRCA continued its boom. In 1997, when Meissner and Reno called in the press to trumpet that year's deportations of 112,000 illegal immigrants, reporters pointed to reports that the nation's illegal immigrant population was increasing dramatically.

USA Today reported that Meissner "could not predict when the stepped-up enforcement efforts would substantially reduce the overall number of illegal immigrants."[86] Said Meissner, "I would not want to speculate on that. I think the important point is that all the trend lines are in the right direction." Janet Reno, using another phrase that became a Clinton administration favorite, declared that the record deportation figures showed the effectiveness of the administration's strategy to establish "a seamless web of enforcement from the border to the workplace." Despite Reno's best intentions, the "seamless web" was a myth that was mocked by the reality of both the border and the worksite.

The Backlash Builds,
but Farmers Call Their Friends

As illegal immigration gathered strength, so did the backlash against it. In 1996, Patrick Buchanan ran for the Republican presidential nomination on a populist platform that foreshadowed the Donald Trump campaign 20 years later. In contrast to Trump, he brought a grace note to his campaign, praising Mexicans as "a good people", but he bluntly declared that illegal immigrants had "no right to break our laws and come into our country and go on welfare and, some of them, commit crimes." Buchanan wanted to unwind trade agreements and vowed to "stop this massive illegal immigration cold."[87]

In many parts of the United States elected officials aligned themselves with public anger, declaring their own frustration with illegal immigration and their determination to stop it. But on the rare occasions when INS agents cracked down on industries that were backbones of local economies, members of Congress switched to ad hoc displays of righteous indignation against the heavy hand of the immigration police. And so it was in 1998, when Bart Szafnicki of the INS office in Atlanta led an operation to arrest dozens of unauthorized Mexican workers who were harvesting Georgia's $80 million Vidalia onion crop.

The farmers of Vidalia had given up on obtaining workers through the H-2A temporary worker program. They complained that the program was too complex and cumbersome. When Szafnicki's men showed up in their fields, the farmers demanded that their elected representatives protect them from financial catastrophe. Congressional offices erupted in responsive outrage. "What the INS has done with Gestapo tactics has been to eliminate the labor supply," said the chief of staff for Republican U.S. Rep Saxby Chambliss.[88]

Another Georgia Republican, U.S. Rep Jack Kingston, was outraged despite his previous alarm at the "explosion of illegal immigrants" and his insistence that "we have no need to apologize for cracking down on those who flout our laws by entering illegally."[89] Kingston joined U.S. Sen. Paul Coverdell and other members of Georgia's congressional delegation in condemning "the apparent lack of regard for farmers in this situation and the intimidation tactics being employed by federal officials." Szafnicki called out a pointed question as Coverdell passed by at a public event. "Can you tell me which laws you passed that you want me to enforce?" he asked.[90]

Pulled between constituents who were usually not organized to press their concerns about illegal immigration and employer groups that were often well organized behind Washington lobbyists, many members of Congress adopted separate strategies for border and interior enforcement. They heaped appropriations on the Border Patrol to demonstrate their determination to defend the rule of law. But on the home front, they protected constituent employers who expected them to intervene with the INS.

David Martin, the INS general counsel from 1995 to 1998, would describe the trend a decade later. Martin observed that "significant interest group pressure quietly helps push Congress toward underfunding these enforcement endeavors, and there has been no equivalently organized constituency pushing back."[91] Efforts to improve the worker verification process "generate determined resistance among a highly influential interest group," Martin wrote. He went on to describe the inclination of Congress to walk the path of least resistance: "Border measures, in contrast, step on almost no influential toes. Border crackdowns are therefore used to demonstrate enforcement seriousness, alienating few and placating many. But focusing only on the border is an ineffective way to master our enforcement problems. The key fulcrum for effectiveness is the workplace."

In a 2017 interview, Martin elaborated on his observation of the behind-the-scenes process by which financial support was drained from worksite enforcement. "We knew that groups like the Chamber of Commerce were well organized and very savvy and had good communications channels with the appropriators," Martin said. "That's where it would show up. It also showed up in internal deliberations, as the president's budget was being put together — what would be funded and what wouldn't — plus the departmental and DOJ decisions as to what they would prioritize."[92]

A prime example of enforcement schizophrenia on Capitol Hill is the 1996 immigration bill, which carried the cumbersome name "The Illegal Immigration Reform and Immigrant Responsibility Act of 1996". The legislation mandated the hiring of thousands of new Border Patrol agents to keep the undocumented out of the country, but it also frustrated efforts to keep them out of the workplace. Moreover, the bill produced something akin to a legislative card trick. While legislators authorized 300 additional INS worksite investigators each year for three years, Republicans in control of the appropriations committees blocked funding for those positions. That prompted Sen. Ted Kennedy to complain that "when it comes to enforcing the immigration laws in the workplace, one has to wonder whether our Republican friends are really serious." [93]

Kennedy's complaint prompted Arizona Republican Jon Kyl to aim an accusatory finger at the White House. Sen. Kyl didn't want Republican fingerprints to be alone on the card trick. He said the Clinton administration had failed to assert its influence on behalf of efforts to boost worksite enforcement. "If there is any blame for not having adequate appropriations, I do not think you can just lay it at the doorstep of Congress," he said. "It is the responsibility of both the administration and the Congress to ensure that in laying out these new challenges and responsibilities we have got to fund it as well as authorize it adequately."[94]

Morale Falls, Raids Diminish

While Meissner and the White House declared their commitment to the rule of law, INS agents in the field remained frustrated at the paucity of resources that Congress provided to deal with a problem that was expanding dramatically across the country. Belying repeated assurances of the Clinton administration's vigilance and determination, the GAO reported that worksite enforcement accounted for less than 4 percent of INS enforcement work in the 1996 fiscal year. Moreover, most arrests produced meager results because, as the Department of Justice's inspector general reported, "INS does not have adequate resources to house and deport most of the illegal aliens it encounters in the worksite."[95]

Morale dwindled. Agents in the field believed INS headquarters was turning its back on worksite enforcement. Tom Fischer, directing the Atlanta office, recalled that at meetings with his peers from other parts of the country, "Everybody would moan and groan" about the lack of support. That assessment was echoed by Bart Szafnicki, who as assistant district director for investigations in Atlanta had worked under Fischer. "It always felt like you had to battle to do your job," Szafnicki said in a 2016 interview. "You were thwarted one way or another. A lot of it was subtle. They would be trying to focus your energies in another direction." He said it was clear that many people at high levels looked askance at those who believed that INS raids were an essential tactic in the effort to deter illegal immigration. "Sometimes it was like they thought you were Don Quixote tilting at windmills."

In the summer of 1996, a worksite raid in Alan Simpson's home state of Wyoming provided a case study of the excess and clumsiness that eroded public support for roundups of illegal immigrant workers. According to a *Denver Post* account about the raid in the tourist town of Jackson Hole, some suspects were "nabbed on the street merely because their skin was brown, while others were loaded into a horse trailer stinking from manure."[96] Although the worst abuses were apparently committed by local police who had assisted in the raid, the resulting uproar tainted the INS, which initiated the operation. Said INS official Joe Greene, "We flubbed it. ...We're not going to do business like that anymore."

As if to demonstrate the futility of the raid, some of the deported workers returned to Jackson a week or two later. One news story told of grim conditions that made Americans shun work there. "American workers won't take those jobs because they don't pay a living wage," said one resident. "Mexicans are willing to live 10 people to a two-bedroom apartment." Another said Mexicans "work lots of overtime for straight pay, and they won't go complaining about it to the labor board."[97]

Syndicated columnist Lars-Erik Nelson used the Jackson Hole episode to criticize IRCA's fatal structural flaw. "The law rewards ignorance," he wrote. "There is virtually no penalty for hiring illegal aliens. All you need is a blank look, a shrug of the shoulders and an innocent, hurt voice when it is suggested your ragged $2-per-hour dishwashers, speaking in unknown tongues, might not be legal residents."[98]

Rising Anger from a Restive Public

Public frustration was commonplace in communities that experienced an intense illegal influx. Sen. Chuck Grassley (R-Iowa) reported on constituent complaints about the seeming inability of the INS to respond to calls for help. Grassley told of a police chief who "had released a truckload of illegals because the INS would not or could not pick them up." INS commissioner Doris Meissner responded that the demand for INS special agents exceeded the agency's supply. "We are moving as quickly as we can, given the staffing that we have," she said. "And as soon as we have more, Iowa is on the list."

Three years later, Congress would provide funding for the INS to station "quick response teams" in Iowa and nine other states where illegal immigration boomed in the 1990s: Arkansas, Colorado, Georgia, Iowa, Kentucky, Missouri, Nebraska, North Carolina, and South Carolina. That effort prompted a warning from labor union organizer Muzaffar Chishti that such cooperation "will do irreparable harm to law enforcement and public safety," because "if local police are known to have a cooperative relationship with the INS, members of immigrant communities are not likely to report crimes or assist officers investigating crimes."[99] And so the tensions grew, steadily compounding in variety and complexity as the illegal influx continued. Enforcement advocates wanted tough measures. Defenders of illegal immigrants warned of the costs of alienating the newcomers. The INS, chronically beleaguered, underfunded, and hounded by critics on all sides, struggled to find its way in a fraught social and political environment.

Sen. Kyl of Arizona, the state that received much of the illegal traffic deflected from California by Operation Gatekeeper, told Meissner that he had received "considerable correspondence" seeking information about the Border Patrol's buildup there.[100]

The Border Patrol added 400 agents between 1996 and 1998, growing to 1,200 in that border state. Meanwhile, the investigative team responsible for monitoring tens of thousands of employers in the vast northern two-thirds of the state was only allowed to grow from six agents to seven. As a result, the agent in charge of investigations, Tony Esposito, said he had to ignore 75 percent of even the most detailed and promising tips brought to his office. "I don't have anybody to assign them to," he said. The headline on the *Arizona Republic* story that reported Esposito's predicament neatly encapsulated the problem: "Illegals on Job Being Ignored: Border Patrol Buildup No Help at Work Sites".[101]

And so, as interior enforcement failed, the rising tide overwhelmed the flimsy barriers set against it.

A Bungled Raid Accelerates the Retreat from the Worksite

Throughout the second half of the 1990s, worksite enforcement was beset by problems old and new. Senator Simpson complained that the INS routinely settled employer sanctions fines for 42 cents on the dollar, thereby undermining the effort to incentivize compliance with the laws."[102] The GAO pointed to problems at the Department of Labor, which had agreed to work with the INS to identify employers who knowingly hired unauthorized workers. The GAO reported that Labor had "generally limited" its cooperation with the INS because it feared that "unauthorized workers fearing possible removal from INS could be discouraged from complaining about labor standards violations."[103] Those labor violations were the DOL's principal responsibility and primary concern.

If a researcher had produced a graph to measure the INS's sagging commitment to worksite enforcement, it would have been the mirror image of a graph tracking the rise in the number of the illegal immigrant population. In 1998, the INS Miami office, for example, investigated only 126 employers, compared to 711 in 1988 when the agency believed it had political support and a mission to shut off the job magnet.[104]

One of those 1998 investigations in Miami culminated in a raid that became infamous for its excesses. It unfolded at a Miami flower wholesaler, First Paragon Floral, where the INS had been alerted to the presence of unauthorized workers. Agents arrested 23 people — from Nicaragua, Honduras, Columbia, Peru, and Chile. Most were unauthorized. But as agents forcefully hustled workers into vans, coworkers screamed — truthfully — that some were authorized. Fights broke out and a larger melee ensued. Agents "commanded workers to sit on a wet floor, then held them in a cooler where flowers are stored at 34 degrees," reported the *Miami Herald*.[105] One woman complained an agent had grabbed her by the hair, knocked her to the ground, and kicked her in the back. Rep. Lincoln Diaz-Balart, a Republican from Miami, was furious at the INS. "They mistreated people," he said. "They pushed and hit."[106] He was joined by Miami-Dade County Mayor Alex Penelas, who said "These people were treated like a herd of cows."[107]

The raid at First Paragon Floral was an enormous embarrassment for the INS. Meissner apologized, and INS headquarters ordered that future raids be directed only at "major violators", which it defined as employers "who intentionally and repeatedly engage in illegal hiring; are involved in other criminal activity, including smuggling and fraud," and those who "hire unauthorized workers and subject them to abusive work conditions."[108] This was a major redirection of resources away from the broad American workplace and toward the narrow band of egregious offenders.

That retreat signaled another trend at the INS. The new constraints on INS worksite enforcement would be fully articulated in an interior enforcement strategy document drafted at the direction of Robert Bach, the INS executive assistant commissioner for policy and planning.

Bach, a sociologist of strong liberal leanings, came to the INS from the State University of New York, Binghamton, where he had been director of the Institute for Research on Multiculturalism and International Labor. In a 1978 research paper titled "Mexican Immigration and the American State", Bach took a deterministic view of U.S. immigration policy, writing that "the American state permitted and indeed had to permit illegal immigration to meet its various commitments to different sectors of capital and labor."[109]

One of Bach's research partners was Doris Meissner. In 1990, while Bach was still at Binghamton and Meissner directed the Immigration Policy Project at the Carnegie Endowment for International Peace, they co-authored an analysis of worksite enforcement that took a less ideological and more pragmatic approach than Bach's earlier paper. They wrote that past experience had demonstrated that employer sanctions could be effective, but only if policy makers committed to "a sustained effort over a period of years and a willingness to adjust law and practice to reflect experience." Echoing a concern that had been repeatedly stated by Barbara Jordan, they wrote, "A generous evolving immigration policy cannot sustain public support in the absence of effective deterrents to illegal immigration."[110]

After Meissner became commissioner, she brought Bach to INS headquarters to help her chart the agency's course. Together they would adjust INS strategy to reflect what they saw as the realities emerging from the growing economic, social, and political imperatives that emerged from the turbulence of the mass illegal immigration of the mid- and late-1990s.

Jack Shaw's Attack on Meissner and Bach

At the end of 1998 Jack Shaw retired from the INS and went public with his frustration with Meissner and Bach at a congressional hearing. It was a strong, if modulated denunciation of their leadership, particularly regarding enforcement of IRCA and other aspects of immigration law. But the hearing was almost entirely ignored by the Washington press. Perhaps reporters were turned off by the hearing's drab title: "Designations of Temporary Protected Status and Fraud in Prior Amnesty Programs".

In his oral testimony to the House Subcommittee on Immigration and Claims, Shaw summarized years of frustrated attempts to interest Meissner in his ideas regarding interior enforcement. He poured out his frustration at what he felt was the marginalization of the investigations division, which he had directed from 1984 to 1995. "I would hope that the Congress ... shares my expectation, and yes, my sense of frustration in waiting for INS senior management to propose, seek funding for, and enthusiastically endorse and implement a cohesive, fully integrated interior enforcement strategy," he said. He concluded with a cry of the heart, calling for INS senior management to recognize "the professional competence, fidelity and dedication of the long-overlooked coterie of special agents of the INS."[111]

The power of Shaw's attack on Meissner and Bach was blunted because he confined his strongest criticism to the written statement he submitted for the record. Even there Shaw's critique was elliptical, as he assessed the influence of the coalition of immigration advocates that Alan Simpson icily referred to as "the groups".

Said Shaw: "Immigration advocacy groups exert a strong interest in areas of INS policy formulation ... and they are not prone to endorse strong enforcement actions away from the land borders to deny aliens immigration benefits." Referring to Bach only by his title, Shaw said that at a strategy planning meeting, "[T]he executive associate commissioner for policy and plans noted that there are operational sensitivities to take into account and no strong public consensus for INS enforcement activities in the interior of the United States." Clearly referring to Meissner and Bach, he said, "INS top management remains reticent and lukewarm" about enforcement.

Shaw also blamed Congress for slighting interior enforcement while lavishing money on the Border Patrol. He drove this point home by inserting in the record an excerpt from an article in the Raleigh *News and Observer*:

> *A raid last March at El Mandado, a Hispanic grocery and cafe in North Raleigh, came after the INS received phone calls about a story in The News & Observer that profiled a store employee and documented his illegal border crossing. Last year, when INS agents charged two Mexicans in Sanford with smuggling deaf countrymen into the United States to sell trinkets, the raid sprang from efforts in New York and elsewhere to break up a larger ring.*
>
> *In reality, the INS still strikes little fear in illegal immigrants here.*
>
> *After leaving his home in Mexico in 1996, Rogelio, 42, now a landscaper in Durham, was caught three times*

in a single month after crossing the Texas border with a smuggler. Yet when he made it to North Carolina on the fourth try, he was in the clear.

"En Carolina del Norte, no hay problemas con La Migra," said Rogelio, who asked that his name be changed for publication. Translation: In North Carolina, immigration authorities pose no problems.

Instead of focusing on states like North Carolina, the INS tends to keep its binoculars focused on the Mexican border.

As Congress boosted the Washington-based agency's budget 163 percent in six years, the enforcement priority has been clear. Each year through 2002, the INS is to deploy an additional 1,000 Border Patrol agents, for a total of 12,000.

Yet almost half the illegal-entry problem has nothing to do with border enforcement. The INS' own statistics show that four of every 10 undocumented immigrants enter the country legally — usually on short-term tourist or work visas — and then stay.[112]

Despite the vivid newspaper account, Shaw's presentation was so subdued and understated that it had little effect. It had the impact of the proverbial tree that falls in the depths of a forest where there is no one to hear it. As a call for public outrage and mobilization on behalf of worksite enforcement, it was a dud. But in his public expression of frustration with INS leadership, Shaw gave voice to the disaffection with Doris Meissner that ran deep among the corps of INS investigators whose duty was to enforce the nation's immigration laws. Meissner had many admirers in and out of the INS, but there were few special agents among them. She declined to be interviewed for this report.

Doris Meissner and the Special Agents

INS investigators, also known as special agents, were immersed in a conservative culture of commitment to the rule of law. They were attuned to the risks and dangers of loose borders, illegal immigration, the plethora of scams used to cheat the system, and the rising threat from international terrorist organizations.

INS Commissioner Doris Meissner, by contrast, was a liberal immigration scholar and Washington technocrat, appreciative of the diversity and dynamism that immigrants bring to the country and alert to the shifting currents of immigration politics. While Meissner understood that law enforcement was essential to the integrity and viability of the immigration system, she was most interested in fulfilling the INS responsibility to attend to those who sought naturalization and other services. Indeed, after taking the reins at the agency, Meissner declared that her goal was to put the "N" back in INS.

"Doris seemed to be uncomfortable with the enforcement side of the house," said Anne Veysey, an analyst in the investigations division during the Clinton administration. "She was much more comfortable with giving than with enforcing." Several agents described Meissner in identical terms, saying that while she was "a nice person", she was "not an enforcement person". Two former supervisory agents, recalling Meissner's visits to investigations offices in Virginia and Phoenix, said she was clearly physically uncomfortable in the agents' presence.

The two cultures clashed in ways both subtle and overt. Veysey recalled documents she had sent to Meissner that came back with the phrase "illegal aliens" scratched out. "We were told that Doris didn't like that," she said. That term had long been used in legal documents, news reports, and research papers to identify those who had violated immigration law, and Meissner herself had used the term in the 1990 research paper she co-authored with Robert Bach. But as time passed, it was increasingly seen as offensive, especially by advocacy groups whose influence grew throughout the 1990s. They preferred the more dignified "undocumented immigrants", a term that conservatives often rejected with the observation that the "undocumented" frequently had multiple sets of fraudulent documents. Meissner was not sympathetic with such reasoning. "She wanted a kinder, gentler immigration service," Veysey said. And so the divide within the INS sometimes presented a microcosm of the broader national debate, which could break down on issues of linguistics well before any discussion of policy.

Gregory Bednarz, the acting assistant commissioner for investigations from 1995 to 2002, still vividly recalls a moment that he says encapsulated Meissner's aversion to enforcement. It came after Meissner and other top-level INS staff attended a 1995 briefing by a CIA analyst who came to INS headquarters. Meissner attended at the suggestion of the INS intelligence division. In an email to Meissner, Bednarz had described it as a "Threat Assessment of Islamic Fundamentalist Groups and Impact upon INS". Bednarz recalled that after the briefing, Meissner dismissed it as "a waste of time".[113] Such moments explain the wry quip that circulated among high-level agents who were detailed temporarily from field offices to INS headquarters. They joked that the experience allowed them to understand what it had been like to live in occupied France during World War II.

A few of the former agents contacted for this report expressed admiration for Doris Meissner. "She was probably the most knowledgeable commissioner we had with respect to the scope of her understanding of immigration, with that hole when it came to immigration enforcement operations," said William Yates. One former enforcement agency executive said the joking references to occupied France began before Meissner's tenure and reflected a long-established cultural divide at the INS. Former INS General Counsel David Martin said the cultural divide between INS law enforcers and a service-oriented commissioner who had to navigate tricky political currents of Capitol Hill was no surprise. Indeed, the weak enforcement regime at the Clinton-era INS may be seen as typifying the style of a president who, according to veteran critic of the Washington establishment Kevin Phillips, "abandoned his populist outsider postures to compromise with established lobbies, power brokers, and congressional leaders."[114]

Under Clinton, the growth of illegal immigration ran a parallel course with the rise of poverty. "Since 1990, about 90 percent of the increase in people living below the government's poverty lines has come among Hispanics," columnist Robert Samuelson would write in 2006. "That has to be mainly immigrants and their U.S.-born children." Citing the difficulties unchecked immigration causes for previous immigrants, Samuelson wrote, "There's a paradox. To make immigration succeed, we need to curb some immigration."[115]

Uproar Over a New Enforcement Strategy

Four days after the hearing where Shaw went public with his frustrations, newspapers published stories about the new INS enforcement strategy that had been written under INS executive Robert Bach's direction. Deportation of criminal aliens would be the number-one priority. In descending order of priority, investigators would also pursue smuggling rings that brought illegal immigrants to the United States, fraudulent efforts to receive immigration benefits such as green cards or other visas, and employers who not only knowingly hired unauthorized workers, but also compounded the offense by abusing them.

The Scripps Howard News Service reported that critics described the plan as "a first step toward amnesty" for illegal immigrants.[116] One of the critics was Jack Shaw. "It is amnesty in another name," said Shaw. "INS is ducking the bullet on the responsibility of providing resources to the field offices to detain and remove" people who were illegally in the country.

More criticism came from an INS official quoted in the story. "This says if you can get in, get a job, and stay out of trouble your chances of being deported are zero," the official said. "You have to wonder about the message it is sending to people thinking about coming here as illegal immigrants." The strategy seemed to contradict an observation Bach and Meissner made in their 1990 analysis of enforcement when they wrote, "Compliance can only be assured over the long run if the enforcement is credible."[117]

The *Washington Post* observed that the new strategy "affords a measure of relief to the estimated 5.5 million illegal immigrants living in the United States and the thousands of businesses that employ them." But reporter William Branigin added that the strategy was "generating intense criticism within the INS and among advocates of a tougher stand on illegal immigration. They say the new policy undermines the INS's commitment to removing illegal aliens, essentially ignoring them as long as they do not commit a crime that brings them to the agency's attention."[118]

Branigin, respected for the depth of his reporting and the breadth of his sources, added this trenchant analysis: "The change ... reflects the political reality that has doomed previous crackdowns on illegal employment. According to INS insiders, neither the Democrats nor the Republicans have demonstrated the political will to seriously reduce the illegal work force, in large part because key constituencies oppose such efforts. On the Democratic side, interior enforcement directed against undocumented workers tends to alienate lawyers, ethnic lobbies, civil rights groups, and, increasingly, unions trying to organize the newcomers. For the Republicans, worksite raids often pose problems because they arouse bitter complaints from business and agricultural interests."

Lamar Smith, chairman of the House immigration subcommittee, was furious at the new strategy and called another hearing to condemn it. "What's the new strategy?" he asked in his opening statement. "It is a bright flashing sign that says to potential illegal aliens: 'Come to the United States. Once you make it, you are home free.'"[119] Bach responded that worksite raids provided too little bang for too many bucks. He noted that in the 1998 fiscal year, the INS had arrested 13,897 illegal immigrants at worksites across the county, or about 45.6 apprehensions per INS investigator work-year. "At that rate, it would take an enormous increase in investigative resources to begin to have an impact on the number of illegal resident workers in the United States," he said.[120] Bach believed that the illegal immigrant population had grown so large that raids were an anachronism, a prohibitively expensive remnant from an earlier time.

Sitting with Bach at the hearing was Mark Reed, the director of the INS's Dallas-based Central Region. As his Exhibit A in support of the new strategy, Reed told the story of one of the largest enforcement operations in INS history, the 1992 raid at a meat processing plant in Grand Island, Neb. "We took about 200 agents, helicopters, K9 groups," Reed said. "We arrested over 300 people at the plant. It got national coverage. And nothing happened. When we went back again this year, that same plant had that many, if not more, unauthorized workers." Seven years on, Reed said, "That is just not a strategy that we have enough [agents] to do."

Operation Vanguard

At the time of that hearing, the new INS strategy was taking dramatic shape in an operation that Reed was directing at worksites across Nebraska. Called Operation Vanguard, it was an effort to shut off the illegal-immigrant employment magnet at every meatpacking plant in the Cornhusker state, which was home to more than 100 of them. The methodology was remarkably simple. After I-9 audits identified about 4,000 apparently unauthorized workers, INS agents scheduled them for interviews to discuss their status. Three thousand of them failed to show up and lost their jobs. The remainder, able to correct errors in their personnel files or INS records, kept working.

The *Wall Street Journal* opened a window on meatpacking in Nebraska with a story about the hiring practices of industry giant IBP.[121] According to the *Journal*, the company hired recruiters who placed radio advertisements that offered wages of $8 an hour, bus transportation to the United States, and health insurance to persons authorized to work in the United States. The fraudulent document industry solved the problem of work authorization for many workers. Some came with counterfeit papers, while others bought or borrowed genuine documents that had been issued to someone else.

Complicating the enforcement challenge for the INS was the recidivism rate among deportees, which was so high it threatened to make a mockery of the time and expense involved in deportations. Many deportees, especially those who had been returned to Mexico, simply made a turn through the border's revolving door and came right back. "It is simply a cat and mouse game to believe that just by apprehending someone and removing them to their country of origin, that you have finished your job," said Bach. "They are coming back." He cited a 1997 study that found that 75 percent of those deported from the Los Angeles County jail system returned to the United States within six years and got into another round of trouble with the criminal justice system.

The counter-argument, making the case for a deportation strategy, also was well represented at the hearing. Former INS agent Thomas Hammond predicted that Operation Vanguard would be futile because the workers it scared out of one job would simply move down the road and find another. The deterrent effect of possible deportation would be lost and word would go out that the coast was clear, he said. "When smuggled illegal aliens are allowed to remain, they announce their success to their friends, relatives, and countrymen; and the result is more smuggled aliens," he said.[122] Adding to the criticism, Robert Hill, an immigration attorney who had served on the Jordan Commission, noted that the commission had endorsed deportation as essential to credible deterrence. Expressing alarm at the new INS strategy, Hill said that in recent months he had observed "the deterioration of a system that appears to be collapsing under its own weight."[123]

Vanguard would collapse under the political and financial weight of the Nebraska meatpacking industry. But to put that development in a larger frame, it is useful to understand how Vanguard came into being. Eric Schlosser provided a taut description of its socio-economic background in his best-selling expose *Fast Food Nation: The Dark Side of the All-American Meal*:

Wrote Schlosser:

> *The industrialization of cattle-raising and meatpacking over the past two decades has completely altered how beef is produced. Responding to the demands of the fast food and supermarket chains, the meatpacking giants have cut costs by cutting wages. They have turned one of the nation's best-paying manufacturing jobs into one of the lowest-paying, created a migrant industrial work-force of poor immigrants, tolerated high injury rates, and spawned rural ghettos in the American heartland. Crime, poverty, drug abuse, and homelessness have lately taken root in towns where you'd least expect to find them. The effects of this new meatpacking regime have become as inescapable as the odors that drift from its feedlots, rendering plants, and pools of slaughter-house waste.*[124]

The Backstory on Operation Vanguard

In a 2017 interview, Mark Reed told the story of the political roots of Operation Vanguard. The story began with an urgent request to the INS from the Nebraska and Iowa delegations in the House of Representatives. They asked Doris Meissner for a meeting to complain about the explosion of illegal immigration in their states. Reed accompanied Meissner to the meeting, where they endured a heated recitation of complaints from towns across the two states.

"They were upset," Reed said, "They said our inability to control the border was adversely affecting their states. It was the old complaint. The schools were being overrun. The health care was being overrun. The judicial system was being overrun. Basically their lifestyle was being overrun because we were unable to stop the flow of people across the border. They were very agitated. If there had been food at that meeting, I think they would have thrown it at us." Reed responded by laying out what became the Operation Vanguard strategy. The congressional offices responded enthusiastically and asked Reed to give them regular updates.

The cheering for Reed's efforts did not last long. Although Vanguard was an operational success, it proved to be a political failure, a repeat in the Northern Plains of the political firestorm that had swept across the onion fields of southern Georgia. The Nebraska meat industry, pointing to the operation's cascading effects for the state's cattle and hog producers, hired former Nebraska Sen. Ben Nelson, a Democrat, to lobby on its behalf. Nelson said it had been "ill-advised for Operation Vanguard to start out in a state with such low unemployment and an already big problem with a shortage of labor."[125] Sen. Chuck Hagel, a Republican, also lined up with the meat industry. And a task force appointed by Gov. Mike Johanns called for an amnesty for unauthorized workers in the state.[126]

It was an intense political backlash on behalf of a dominant industry whose excesses had provoked a populist backlash. Meissner got the word to Reed. "She told me we would have to rethink Vanguard," Reed said in 2017. "I knew then that it was dead."

And so instead of taking Vanguard on the road, the INS put it on ice. And instead of demonstrating the commitment of the federal government to respond to grassroots public concerns by enforcing IRCA, Vanguard demonstrated the futility of a crackdown on a powerful industry when that industry has become accustomed to access to unauthorized workers. The INS response brought to mind the observation of Grover Norquist that in Washington, "intensity trumps preference." In other words, diffuse public opinion is no match for a powerful lobby.

In the absence of systematic and sustained enforcement, illegal immigrants continued to make the dangerous border crossing, heading for Nebraska and many other parts of the country. One metric of the influx came from the desert mountains of the Border Patrol's Tucson Sector, where arrests reached 616,000 in 2000, up from 139,000 in 1994.[127]

In late 2000 as the Clinton presidency neared its end, Doris Meissner resigned as commissioner of the Immigration and Naturalization Service. She later helped establish the Migration Policy Institute, a respected research organization whose work tends to support an expansive immigration policy. She is an advocate of the comprehensive immigration reform legislation that would provide sweeping legalization for illegal immigrants, boost legal immigration, and provide employers with ready access to low-wage workers from abroad.

Doris Meissner and a Caller from Minot, N.D.

In 2007, as the Senate neared a vote on comprehensive reform legislation, Meissner said it would provide a more effective enforcement regime than was possible under IRCA. Then she made what amounted to a repudiation of her claim at a 1996 Senate hearing that under President Clinton "the INS is showing that it means business when it comes to enforcing immigration laws in the workplace." Seven years after leaving government service, Meissner acknowledged, "We never really did in any serious way the enforcement that was to accompany the legalization of the people who were here illegally."[128]

Six years later, when comprehensive reform proposals returned in slightly different form in the so-called Gang of Eight bill, Meissner appeared on C-SPAN to support the proposal for a sweeping legalization coupled with fines and other requirements. "We are talking about accountability — on the part of the people who violated the law by being here illegally as well as by the society overall for having allowed this for so many years," she said.

Then a caller — Phil from Minot, North Dakota — identified himself as the owner of a construction business and made an anguished and angry case that it was the government that should be called to account.

Said Phil: "You have people in this country trying to run their businesses legally. They pay their taxes. They pay their workers compensation. They pay their insurance. And you have other businesses hiring illegal immigrants. They hire them. They know they can't cover them with insurance. They pay them less money and they don't cover them with workers comp. They don't cover them with liability insurance. So they can bid the job way cheaper than anybody running their business legally. If you're running your business legally, you're not hiring illegal immigrants. So I don't hire illegal immigrants. ... So I have to bid my job to cover my expenses in this country. So I am going out of business because you guys are allowing people to hire illegal immigrants. ... And they're really damaging this country. I don't understand how people cannot see this. I mean they are putting me out of business because I won't work illegal immigrants."

Meissner responded: "You know, you are describing very vividly what our dilemma as a country and as a society is. It is why immigration reform is so urgent. This is an unacceptable situation. It's an unacceptable situation for exactly the reasons you described. It creates a completely uneven field in labor markets, particularly in sectors like the construction sector. So we have to get ahold of it. But politically, it has not been possible for the Congress to come to an agreement. The only institution in our society that can resolve this is the Congress, by putting a new system of laws into place."

As Meissner well understood, business interests like those that resisted IRCA in the 1980s and that fought worksite enforcement in the 1990s are a mighty obstacle to such an effort. In 1981, when Meissner was the acting commissioner of the INS and Congress was beginning the debate that ultimately led to passage of IRCA, she testified at a Senate hearing that although an employer sanctions law was needed to stem illegal immigration, "implementation of the law is not designed to be and will not be anti-employer."[129]

Testifying at the same hearing, Cornell University labor economist Vernon Briggs said one benefit of employer sanctions legislation was that it "sets the moral tone. ... that it is an illegal act for an employer to hire an illegal alien." Briggs then added the admonition that "there is not much sense in going through with the employer sanctions if you are not going to have some kind of credible identification system linked with it."[130]

In 1986 Congress managed to pass a law, but after efforts to establish a credible system had been thwarted. Credibility was sacrificed in the name of compromise and for the benefit of intensely organized special interests.

A Labor Movement Landmark in Minneapolis

Another major chapter in the erosion of worksite enforcement began to unfold in the fall of 1999, when workers at a Minneapolis Holiday Inn Express supported a union organizing effort. Hotel management, claiming to have just become aware of their illegal status, fired them and called the INS.

After the workers were arrested, the gambit backfired. The union organized protests. The Equal Employment Opportunity Commission and the National Labor Relations Board sued the employers for retaliatory firing and won a financial settlement for the workers, who were allowed to stay in the country.[131] The story received national attention and became a major factor in the decision of the AFL-CIO's executive council in 2000 to call for an end to employer sanctions and for a blanket amnesty for illegal immigrants. That historic move was the lead story on the front page of the *Washington Post*, whose headline announced, "Unions Reverse On Illegal Aliens".[132]

Former INS General Counsel Alex Aleinikoff noted with apparent surprise a comment that Robert Bach had made about the state of worksite enforcement. Bach told the *New York Times* that unauthorized workers ran little risk of arrest "unless the employer turns a worker in, and employers usually do that only to break a union or prevent a strike or that kind of stuff."[133] Retorted Aleinikoff, "That, of course, is precisely the AFL-CIO's complaint. Employer sanctions have not kept undocumented immigrants out of the workplace, and unscrupulous employers rarely face penalties. Instead, the law has provided employers with a justification for firing workers engaged in union activity."

A week after the AFL-CIO's dramatic policy shift, the National Immigration Forum sponsored a panel discussion on the state of the immigration policy debate. The participants, all allies in the battle for legislation to grant legal status to illegal immigrants, noted with satisfaction the changes in the political panorama since the early 1990s. Three observations provide a metric of how far the forces opposed to immigration enforcement had advanced in the 1990s:[134]

- Cecilia Munoz of the National Council of La Raza cited "record numbers of naturalizations" among Latino voters as part of the encouraging shift. She said that in that year's presidential campaign, "the candidates have responded to these changes in the electorate by paying their respect to Latino voters and to immigrant voters."

- Muzaffar Chishti of the Union of Needletrades, Industrial and Textile Employees (UNITE) hailed the AFL-CIO's decision to stop resisting illegal immigrants and recruit them instead. He said the move signaled a recognition of new realities, including the fact that in some areas of the country, "about one-half to three-fourths of new entrants into the low wage labor market are immigrants."

- John Gay, a lobbyist for the American Hotel and Lobbying Association, said, "The greatest problem we face is that we cannot find the number we need of essential workers, as we call them, the lesser skilled and unskilled workers." Gay was co-chair of an organization formed by the Chamber of Commerce and low-wage employers — in such fields as hotels, restaurants, nursing homes, and home building — who were pushing for comprehensive immigration reform. It was called the Essential Worker Immigration Coalition (EWIC). The name was an exercise in irony. It showed workers more respect than their paychecks offered. Gay's duties on Capitol Hill included lobbying against legislation to raise the federal minimum wage.

Low wages, of course, are a function of loose labor markets. As the U.S. jobless rate dipped to 4 percent in 2000, EWIC sought to loosen labor markets. In a letter to members of Congress, it said, "The global workforce market should be more readily available to businesses in order to meet workforce needs."[135]

Backlash and Another View of the Worksite Fait Accompli

A 2000 article in *Foreign Affairs* magazine made a case for resisting employers' efforts to loosen labor markets by providing visas to foreign workers. It reported that the intense immigration of the 1990s was "creating special burdens and tensions" in states from California and Arizona to New Jersey. It quoted Georgetown University immigration expert Susan Martin, who had been the executive director of the Jordan Commission. In its reports to Congress, the commission predicted that when the economy sagged, the country could expect a backlash "that could be greater than it was in California." The article concluded with a warning: "If Congress and the next president do not come up with reasonable solutions along the lines proposed by the Jordan Commission, the field will be clear for the unreasonable solutions advanced by politicians such as Pete Wilson and Pat Buchanan."[136]

The following year, *New York Times* reporter Louis Uchitelle took his own measure of INS enforcement work. "The agency now concentrates on picking up aliens who have committed a crime," he reported. "The rest are in effect allowed to help American employers fill jobs." His story included this anodyne observation by Robert Bach on the jobs panorama opened up by INS inattention at the workplace: "It's just the market at work, drawing people to jobs, and the INS has chosen to concentrate its actions on aliens who are a danger to the community."

Uchitelle reported that leniency at the INS helped explain why the economy had registered smaller pay increases than economists had expected in the tight labor market of the time. The wage-suppressing effect drew the approval of Alan Greenspan of the Fed because it helped keep a lid on inflation. Greenspan, perhaps the country's most famous libertarian, smiled approvingly at the economic effects of mass immigration.

Liberal economist Jared Bernstein would note a less benign consequence. Bernstein said illegal immigration contributed to what he called an economic "crunch" suffered by American workers. Unlike Greenspan and Robert Bach, Bernstein didn't think it was a good idea to sit back and let employers have access to workers from around the world for whom an American minimum wage represented a major upgrade. Taking the classic liberal stance in defense of American workers, Bernstein wrote what amounted to a lament of the policies of the federal government:

> *I hate to go to the Big Brother place. But we need to get between employers addicted to an endless flow of cheap labor and unauthorized immigrants for whom a substandard job here is a step up. We have the technology to implement a reliable system that tells employers whether they're hiring an illegal worker. What we have lacked thus far is the political guts to mete out serious punishment to those employers who ignore the law.*[137]

3. The George W. Bush Years

When Texas Governor George W. Bush ran for president in 2000, he often talked respectfully of those who entered the United States illegally in search of work. "Family values do not stop at the Rio Grande," he said. "If you're a mother or dad and you can't find work close to home, and you're worth your salt, you're coming."[138] Bush's genial rhetoric was an expression of the "compassionate conservatism" that was the theme of his campaign. It was also a sharp departure from the alarm in his party just four years earlier. The 1996 Republican platform declared that "illegal immigration has reached crisis proportions."[139]

After Bush became president, his choice to be commissioner of the INS was James Ziglar, a former banker and a libertarian in the business-friendly, and open-borders tradition of the *Wall Street Journal.* Ziglar was a frequent contributor to the Republican Party and a boyhood friend of Sen. Trent Lott (R-Miss). His background, including a stint as sergeant at arms of the Senate, provoked skepticism about his qualifications to run the INS. An editorial in the *San Diego Union Tribune* scoffed, "He is, to put it politely, a purely political appointee."[140]

The INS became the object of ridicule when it was revealed that six months after the terrorist attacks of September 11, the agency had approved student visas that allowed two of the 9/11 terrorists to attend flight school in Florida. Ziglar's term at the INS would be cut short by the political fallout from those attacks. His libertarian sensibility was out of tune with the times. Barely a year after coming to the INS, Ziglar resigned.

The staff report of the 9/11 Commission criticized the INS for failure to understand the national security implications of its work. "Prior to September 11, immigration inspectors were focused on facilitating the entry of travelers to the United States," the report observed. "Special agents were focused on criminal aliens and alien smuggling, and those handling immigration benefits were inundated with millions of applications. Thus, on the eve of the 9/11 attacks, the INS found itself in a state of disarray."[141]

The staff report also highlighted the cultural and ideological breech at the INS that became pronounced during the tenure of Doris Meissner. As we have seen, Meissner's chilly relationship with the INS investigations division was exemplified by her dismissal of a 1995 CIA briefing on terrorism as "a waste of time". The staff of the 9/11 Commission provided another indication that Meissner regarded terrorism as irrelevant. It reported that in a 2003 interview that "Meissner did not recall the briefing and "told us she never heard of Usama Bin Ladin until August 2001, nearly 10 months after she left the INS."[142]

Mexico Deal Goes Down, Border Patrol Builds Up

Another casualty of 9/11 attacks was President Bush's immigration-policy initiative with Mexican President Vicente Fox. The two leaders, both elected in 2000, quickly developed what news reports touted as a "dos amigos" relationship. It was aimed at opening the border to a freer flow of Mexican labor and providing legal status to Mexicans living and working illegally in the United States. After the 9/11 attacks, those ideas were put on hold.

Meanwhile, the flow of illegal immigration remained intense despite the Border Patrol buildup ordered by Congress. In 2002, the Public Policy Institute of California reported that it found "no statistically significant relationship between the build-up and the probability of migration. Economic opportunities in the United States and Mexico have a stronger effect on migration than does the number of agents at the border."[143]

A central premise of the Immigration Reform and Control Act was that worksite enforcement would shut off the job magnet that attracted illegal immigration. But instead of correcting the defects that energized the magnet with fraud, Congress bankrolled a multi-billion-dollar border-industrial complex, with contractors competing to provide surveillance cameras mounted on towers, mobile surveillance units, ground sensors, unmanned aircraft to supplement a regular air force of helicopters and planes, border fencing illuminated by stadium lights, and fleets of new four-wheel drive trucks. From a force of 3,200 when IRCA was passed, the Border Patrol grew to nearly 10,000 agents in 2001, on its way to 19,000 by the end of the Bush presidency.

The Creation of ICE

Following passage of the Homeland Security Act of 2002, the law enforcement responsibilities of the INS and the Customs Service were merged under the Department of Homeland Security. Then those responsibilities were divided between two new agencies, Customs and Border Protection and the Bureau of Immigration and Customs Enforcement, which is now known as Immigration and Customs Enforcement, or ICE. Within ICE, the Homeland Security Investigations division handles not only legacy INS duties such as worksite enforcement and pursuit of smuggling and benefits fraud, but also the legacy Customs responsibilities in such areas as drug trafficking, cybercrime, money laundering, intellectual property theft, and enforcement of export laws.

The ICE merger was not a happy union. Agents from "legacy INS" regarded it as a hostile takeover in which Customs imposed its will, showing little regard for those who had sought to enforce immigration laws. "The organization is stagnated in a convolution of identities and cultures brought over from INS and Customs," ICE official Philip Wrona acknowledged. He wrote that many legacy INS agents, feeling disdained and dominated by legacy Customs, sought work elsewhere. He noted their complaints "that they are continually demeaned when they hear legacy Customs agents refusing to perform INS enforcement work because it is not real criminal enforcement work." Wrona quoted a legacy INS employee at ICE as saying, "We hear from the legacy Customs ... [that] 'we'll be a lot better off when we get rid of this immigration shit.'"[144]

The Government Accountability Office, which had long pointed with urgent concern to the structural flaws of INS worksite enforcement, maintained its vigilance after the Department of Homeland Security took charge of ICE. It reported that worksite enforcement in the post-9/11 era was constrained by "limited resources and competing priorities for those resources".

Priority number one was national security. Indeed, ICE issued a memo requiring field offices to request approval from headquarters before investigating any worksite not related to "critical infrastructure", such as airports and nuclear power plants.[145] While that rule was later relaxed, the GAO reported, "Eight of the 12 offices we interviewed told us that worksite enforcement was not an office priority unless the worksite enforcement case related to critical infrastructure protection." According to the GAO, in 1999, the INS had devoted about 9 percent of its agents work-years to worksite enforcement, but in 2003, worksites received only 4 percent of agents' work years.[146]

The Expanding Dimensions of Crime

Against this background of listless enforcement, the illegal immigrant population continued to surge, thereby expanding the dimensions of the enforcement challenge in what became a self-propelled downward spiral of illegality. In a report titled "Numerous Daunting Enforcement Issues Facing ICE," the GAO reported that:

> *The number of individuals smuggled into the United States has increased dramatically, and alien smuggling has become more sophisticated, complex, organized, and flexible. Thousands of aliens annually illegally seek immigration benefits, such as work authorization and change of status, and some of these aliens use these benefits to enable them to conduct criminal activities. Hundreds of thousands of aliens unauthorized to work in the United States have used fraudulent documents to circumvent the process designed to prevent employers from hiring them. In many instances, employers are complicit in this activity.*[147]

That report was one of several candid official acknowledgements of the alarming dimensions of the challenge to law enforcement. The Justice Department, for example, describing the nexus between immigration and the proliferation of drug trafficking, reported that in the Washington-Baltimore area, "the dramatic increase in the Hispanic population has enabled Colombian, Dominican, and, increasingly, Mexican, Guatemalan, and Salvadoran criminal groups and gangs with ties to drug source and transit countries to operate more easily."[148]

Another reason that ICE agents were spending such little time at the worksite was that they were occupied with more direct threats to public welfare. They conducted Operation Cross

Check to deport violent offenders and members of transnational gangs. Operation Soar (Sex Offender Alien Removal) targeted those who had been convicted of sex offenses. The *Baltimore Sun* reported that Operation Predator had led to the arrest of "more than two dozen illegal immigrants and green-card holders who have criminal sex-offense records."[149]

Along the Arizona Border

In the early years of the Bush administration, the Border Patrol detailed hundreds of agents — at tremendous expense for motel lodging alone — to the Arizona border, which included the most active smuggling corridors. By 2004, the Patrol's Tucson sector had 2,200 agents, up from 287 a decade earlier. But even a force that size could not control the sector's 261 miles of border.

In 2005, the author met a 28-year-old Mexican outside Phoenix who was surprised at how easy it had been to come across near Nogales. He said he had been part of a small group that was led by a smuggler who charged $1,100 for a two-hour hike through the desert to a rendezvous with a car that took him to Phoenix. "Next time I'll do it myself," he said as he stood on a street, hoping to be picked up by a contractor for a day's work.

To be sure, the risk of arrest at the border was rising. In 2005 the Border Patrol arrested 1,600 illegal crossers every night. But agents acknowledged that for every one they arrested, two to four others got away. Some smuggling organizations, handling hundreds of people per week, adopted the strategy of deliberately sending a group of 15 or 20 toward Border Patrol agents. They knew that for the next several hours while the agents were processing and transporting their clients, the way would be clear for other groups to make it through to rendezvous points with a smuggler's vehicles. They also knew the migrants who had been used to distract the Border Patrol would soon be released into Mexico, where they could rest before crossing again in a day or two.

A single table in a report from the Congressional Research Service is the statistical equivalent of a smoking gun in the case against the Bush administration's commitment to enforcement. It showed that in contrast to 1999, when federal agents initiated 443 fines against employers for hiring unauthorized workers, they issued 16 in 2003. Criminal cases dropped from 109 in 1999 to four in 2003. During the same four-year period, fines collected from offending employers declined from $3.6 million to $212,000.[150]

Table 1. Worksite Enforcement Program Performance, FY 1999 - FY2003

Fiscal Year	1999	2000	2001	2002	2003
Criminal Employer Cases Presented for Prosecution	182	109	239	21	4
Notices of Intent to Fine (NIFs) Issued	443	213	141	73	16
Fine Amounts Collected	$3.6 m	$2.2 m	$1.6 m	$509 k	$212 k

Source: Adapted from Alison Siskin, Andorra Bruno, Blas Nunez-Neto, Lisa M. Seghetti, and Ruth Ellen Wasem, "Immigration Enforcement Within the United States", Congressional Research Service, August 6, 2006, p. 41.

Such hard facts about soft enforcement presented a problem of political staging for the Bush White House, which was energetically promoting immigration reform legislation sponsored in the Senate by Republican John McCain and Democrat Edward Kennedy. Much like IRCA in 1986, their legislation promised to match legalization for illegal immigrants with worksite enforcement to prevent future waves of illegal immigration. But the Bush administration's record of feckless enforcement at the worksite created a credibility gap as vast as the Mexican border.

An Enforcement Offensive

In the spring of 2006, ICE launched a campaign to demonstrate its newly found enforcement bona fides. During the 12 months from April 2006 to March 2007, agents conducted a dozen major worksite operations. They went big and bold at the outset, with the largest single worksite enforcement action ever taken — coordinated raids at 40 locations of IFCO Systems, a pallet manufacturing company. It resulted in the arrest of seven current and former managers as well as 1,187 unauthorized workers. More than half the company's workforce had used Social Security numbers that were either fake or belonged to someone else. IFCO eventually agreed to pay $20.7 million in civil forfeitures and penalties for the massive fraud.[151]

Later that year ICE agents arrested nearly 1,300 workers at Swift meat-processing plants in Iowa, Minnesota, Nebraska, Colorado, Utah, and Texas. Those raids highlighted the industry's reliance on unauthorized workers to sustain a business model that had begun years earlier and steadily brutalized the worksite. The model began with the relocation of plants from big cities to rural areas and the replacement of skilled butchers with less-skilled workers who would make the same repetitive cuts thousands of times a day on the dangerous and rapidly moving "disassembly line". Severe wage reductions were another key ingredient. Government data showed that in 2006 wages in the industry were 45 percent lower than they had been in 1980, adjusted for inflation.[152]

In between those two major enforcement actions, President Bush took up the task of assuring the public that his administration was ready to build on IRCA's promise and redeem its failings. "A comprehensive reform bill must hold employers to account for the workers they hire," Bush told the U.S. Chamber of Commerce in a speech its headquarters, which is located directly across Lafayette Park from the White House. "It is against the law to hire someone who is in the country illegally. Those are the laws of the United States of America, and they must be upheld."[153]

The *Washington Post* cast doubt on the president's commitment, raising the suggestion of political expedience as it cited data from the Government Accountability Office. The *Post* reported that despite the administration's vow to crack down at the worksite, it had "virtually abandoned such employer sanctions before it began pushing to overhaul U.S. immigration law."[154]

In an attempt to show that he understood public frustration in Arizona — then ground zero of illegal immigration — Bush sent 6,000 National Guard troops to the border. He called for more detention facilities to hold those arrested by the Border Patrol while they were processed for deportation. And he declared that worksite enforcement must be so tough that it would "leave employers with no excuse for violating" the law.

A Call to Get Serious Beyond the Border

Silvestre Reyes, who became El Paso's Democratic congressman after retiring from the Border Patrol, was not impressed with the rhetoric or the headline-grabbing call-up of the National Guard. Reyes believed that what was needed was a sustained crackdown on rogue employers. He had been chief of the Border Patrol in McAllen, Texas, when IRCA was passed in 1986, and his agents had been part of the earliest employer sanctions work. As word filtered through Mexico that the United States was getting serious, Reyes said, apprehensions in his area dropped by as much as 80 percent.

Reyes had earned his borderlands credibility. His success as the architect of the 1994 Operation Hold the Line, a show of Border Patrol force that imposed order on the chaotic line between El Paso and Juarez, had launched his political career. After Bush's speech, Reyes insisted that a determined commitment to worksite enforcement would enable it to work again. "It would have been much more effective had he announced he was directing the secretary of Homeland Security to identify 1,000 agents that would fan out throughout the country and start doing employer sanctions," he said.[155]

The New Bedford Raid

The risks inherent in aggressive worksite enforcement were highlighted by a 2007 ICE raid on a manufacturing plant in New Bedford, Mass., that produced accessories such as ammunition belts, rucksacks, and other gear for the U.S. military and other customers.

Federal agents arrested 361 of the company's workers, mostly from Guatemala, Honduras, and El Salvador. Prosecutors then charged the owners with conspiring to hire illegal immi-

82

grants, helping them obtain fraudulent docu~
to train them to handle dangerous chemica'   m-
News accounts told of other abuses, includir
conditions and fines for taking bathroom bı
two minutes. There was even an alleged sch
ers overtime pay by issuing separate checкs ᴖ ᴖ
they had worked for two companies.[156] Such was life when illegal workers were afraid to complain about illegal employers.

Critics condemned the New Bedford raid as excessive and
cruel, especially for children who were left on their own after
their parents were arrested. An ICE spokesman insisted that
the agency's efforts to avoid such situations had been frustrated when the parents didn't truthfully answer agents' questions.
There were misunderstandings all around, perhaps inevitable
under the turbulent circumstances of a raid that was intended
to remove unauthorized workers from their jobs and from the
country.

Sen. Kennedy said worksite raids in general "unfairly penalize
vulnerable workers."[157] Other critics were less measured. In an
op-ed column for the *Boston Globe*, two officials of the American Civil Liberties Union likened ICE tactics to a campaign
of ethnic cleansing. "The United States went to war to stop
Slobodan Milosevic's attempt to 'ethnically cleanse' Kosovo in
1999," they wrote. "We should ask ourselves how, just eight
years later, we came to be carrying out a policy that involves
such similar tactics — lightning raids, mass arrests, packed detention centers, and mass deportations."[158]

DHS Secretary Michael Chertoff acknowledged the raid's con-
nection to the push for the immigration reform bill. "I believe
the credibility of [DHS] as a partner in immigration reform is
enhanced by our determination to enforce our immigration
laws firmly as well as fairly," he said.[159] Chertoff's statement

have been an accurate reflection of his intentions. But it ~~few~~ in the face of two decades of federal failure that undermined both the integrity of the law and public confidence that the federal government was serious about enforcement.

"The American People Feel Like They Were Scammed"

In the summer of 2007, the comprehensive reform bill failed in the Senate, collapsing under the weight of a populist uprising that signaled widespread public frustration with illegal immigration. One of the most pointed acknowledgements of that frustration had come earlier, in a Senate hearing that was titled "Immigration Enforcement at the Worksite: Learning from the Mistakes of 1986". There, Texas Republican John Cornyn described IRCA's legacy of governmental failure and public disillusionment.

"The American people feel like they were scammed the last time we were on this subject 20 years ago," said Cornyn. He went on to sum up concerns that had accumulated for two decades. "I feel very strongly that, unless we are serious about making the system work and we actually appropriate the money, hire the people, train the people, actually put them in place, create the databases, and create the secure identification card to make this work, we will find ourselves here once again, with not 12 million people illegally in the United States but maybe 24 million or more," he said.[160]

A few weeks earlier, Doris Meissner made a similar assessment of the requirements of credible enforcement if comprehensive reform were to be passed. "There will need to be not only massive infusions of resources," she said on C-SPAN. "There will need to be a great deal more management acumen, a great deal more administrative skill and commitment devoted to implementing these reforms. These reforms involve enormous workload challenges."[161]

The Growers' Sense of Entitlement

The failure of enforcement is an expression of political expedience. It allows Congress to satisfy both the public clamor for border security and the demands of organized business interests for access to a large supply of cheap labor. In 2016, Stewart Baker, who was the DHS assistant secretary for policy development under George W. Bush, described his meeting with growers who asserted with smug satisfaction that the federal government's policies had protected their access to unauthorized workers. Said Baker, "They introduced themselves along the lines of 'We hire illegal workers illegally; that's what we do, and the system allows it, and we depend on it.'"[162]

The growers' sense of entitlement and the political might they muster have long been powerful shapers of immigration enforcement policies. For many years, the labor demands of agriculture in the West and South were the tail wagging the dog of immigration enforcement policies. In 1951, 35 years before IRCA was passed, the *New York Times* reported the complaint by three INS officers "that a powerful 'pressure group' of farmers annually was forcing suspension of law enforcement against illegal Mexican immigrants in order to get cheap labor."[163] In the 31 years since IRCA was passed, a reliance on illegal-immigrant labor has become characteristic of other sectors of the economy. That entrenchment, along with the growing importance of ethnic political organizations, explains why Congress has shown little interest in providing the resources necessary for credible worksite enforcement. Instead, the nation's lawmakers have sought to placate and pacify the public with ritualistic calls to secure the border and enormous expenditures on the Border Patrol.

In 1985, when Robert Bach was a college professor, he described a leftist theoretical perspective on such an enforcement regime in a capitalist society. Identifying the native U.S. working class as members of the dominant social group, he wrote: "Employing migrants from culturally and racially distinct origins is identified here as a common strategy used by the employer class against organizations of domestic workers. Hence, the benefits brought about by a subordinate minority in the labor market accrue not to all members of the dominant group, but only to members of the employer class. Such benefits are extracted precisely against the interests of the domestic proletariat, which is pitted against the new sources of labor."[164]

Richard Stana of the GAO offered a more pragmatic assessment of the problem. For years Stana, whose organization serves as a watchdog for Congress, attempted to prod Congress to get serious about worksite enforcement. As he put it with characteristic understatement at a congressional hearing, "Achieving an appropriate balance between border and interior enforcement resources could help create a credible framework for deterring those considering illegal entry and overstay."[165]

4. The Obama Years

In 2006, when Sen. Barack Obama was contemplating a run for the White House, he published *The Audacity of Hope: Thoughts on Reclaiming the American Dream.* Obama wrote of "the classic immigrant story" he saw still unfolding as "the story of ambition and adaptation, hard work and education, assimilation and upward mobility."[166]

Yet Obama also sounded a cautionary note. He said mass migration from Latin America had roiled labor markets and stoked understandable resentment in broad swaths of the American public. Noting the tensions that had arisen between blacks and Latinos in his hometown of Chicago, he wrote:

> *There's no denying that many blacks share the same anxieties as many whites about the wave of illegal immigration flooding our Southern border — a sense that what's happening now is fundamentally different from what has gone on before. ... If this huge influx of mostly low-skill workers provides some benefits to the economy as a whole ... it also threatens to depress further the wages of blue-collar Americans and put strains on an already overburdened safety net.*[167]

During his 2008 campaign for the presidency, Obama's pursuit of the Latino vote included a speech to the National Council of La Raza's annual convention. There, as he pledged to make immigration reform "a top priority in my first year as president," he criticized the Bush administration's frequent use of worksite raids. He highlighted in vivid detail the excesses that had marred some of the operations launched by ICE special agents. Something is amiss, Obama said, "when communities are terrorized by ICE immigration raids, when nursing mothers are torn from their babies, when children come home from school to find their parents missing, when people are detained without access to legal counsel."[168]

Another Obama objection to Bush's policies was that they often resulted in the deportation of illegal workers while leaving illegal employers untouched. And so, shortly after he became president, Obama came under pressure from immigration advocates furious that ICE agents in Bellingham, Wash., had raided a plant that rebuilt car engines. They arrested 25 illegal immigrants from Mexico, Guatemala, and El Salvador and processed them for deportation. "What are Latino and immigrant voters to think?" complained the executive director of the National Immigration Forum. "They turn out in massive numbers and vote for change and yet 'Change We Can Believe In' turns out to be business as usual."[169]

Homeland Security Secretary Janet Napolitano stepped in to calm the storm. She publicly rebuked ICE for the raid. Soon the workers were not only released, they were also granted work permits so that they could help prosecutors make the case against their former employers.

Two months after the Bellingham raid, ICE rolled out an enforcement strategy that targeted rogue employers. Much like the policy of the late-Clinton-era INS, it prioritized the prosecution of the worst illegal employers — those who not only made hiring unauthorized workers part of their business plan but also mistreated the workers or schemed with smugglers to bring them in.

This was the centerpiece of what Obama called "a more thoughtful approach than just raids of a handful of workers". *Nation's Restaurant News*, a trade publication, got the word out. "ICE agents are encouraged to prosecute employers after finding evidence of mistreatment of workers, trafficking, smuggling, harboring, visa fraud, document fraud, and other violations," it reported.[170] And so the word went out: The de facto threshold for enforcement had been raised well above the de jure standard established in 1986.

Taking Account of the Obama Worksite Strategy

The most important tool of the new strategy was an old IRCA enforcement stand-by that had become so prominent in Operation Vanguard: audits of the I-9 form that employers were required to have on file for each new worker. Janet Napolitano said the audits, sometimes called "silent raids", were aimed at illegal immigration's demand side. Soon she was boasting that ICE in the Obama era was racking up far more audits and imposing more fines than it had during the Bush administration.

Indeed, the 2,196 worksite audits ICE carried out in 2010 quadrupled the Bush administration's 2008 tally. And in 2013, the most active year of the Obama era, ICE boosted that number to 3,127.[171] But the numbers on the worksite enforcement scoreboards of both administrations represent a tiny fraction of 1 percent of the nation's employers.

They also provide a metric of the decline of enforcement over the years since IRCA. In 1990, for example, the INS not only conducted 5,118 audits, it also carried out 9,588 investigations based on leads about suspected violations.[172] The GAO then tracked a steady decline in the number of lead-driven investigations, which dropped to 5,767 in 1993.

ICE director John Morton said the agency was imposing "smart, tough employer sanctions to even the playing field for employers who play by the rules."[173] But enforcement in the Obama era affected no more than a tiny portion of the vast field of the American workplace, which employed more than seven million unauthorized workers. Since the late 1990s, worksite enforcement has been comparable to a highway patrol policy to issue speeding tickets only to the most egregiously defiant drivers — those who not only exceed the speed limit, but also career recklessly down the highway

A Struggle Over Deportations

The Obama strategy renewed an old debate with Lamar Smith. The Republican congressman from Texas argued that robust deportation was essential to a deterrence strategy to demonstrate that illegal immigration would not be tolerated. Smith also believed that a failure to remove unauthorized workers was a betrayal of American workers. "Seven million people are working in the United States illegally," Smith said. "These jobs should go to legal workers, and securing these jobs for Americans and legal immigrant workers should be a priority of the federal government."[174]

Obama's decision to target illegal employers rather than the workers they hired was consistent with his hopes to sign legislation that would grant legal status to millions of illegal immigrants. In the meantime, however, the administration had the duty to enforce the laws that were still on the books. This presented a dilemma that Morton wrestled with in public. "We've got to have some sort of balanced reform that gets us back to very meaningful enforcement, where the rules do matter and there's integrity in the system," Morton said. "And at the same time we have a very firm but fair means for people who have been here a very long time to gain some sort of path to citizenship."[175]

No enforcement issue was more delicate for John Morton and the White House than deportation. Congressional appropriations bills had given the executive branch a legislative mandate to carry out 400,000 deportations annually. All illegal immigrants were, by definition, subject to deportation unless they received special consideration from the courts or Congress. This was an awkward circumstance for a president whose advocacy of sweeping legalization had helped him win 70 percent of the Hispanic vote in 2008. His response was a two-fold strategy.

First, Obama invoked prosecutorial discretion to target high-priority offenders, including violent criminals, persons who re-entered the country after being deported, and recently arrived illegal immigrants. This would have the effect of shielding those who had established themselves in the United States and stayed away from additional legal trouble. Such persons are sometimes described has having established "equities" in U.S. society.

Second, the administration cooked the books of deportation accounting. Many of those counted as deportees had been arrested near the border and speedily returned to Mexico. Historically, such offenders had been classified as "returns" as opposed to "removals", which are reported as deportations. Obama would himself acknowledge that in the official tallies of deportations "the statistics are a little deceptive."[176]

It was a massive effort, facilitated by an industrial-scale expansion of the detention program ordered by Congress, which between 2006 and 2012 financed an increase in detention bed-spaces from 27,500 to 34,000.[177] Many of the deportations began with a controversial program called Secure Communities, which used fingerprinting in local jails to notify ICE about criminals subject to deportation. By 2013, Secure Communities was established in communities across the country, infuriating immigration advocates who said that it was being used as a dragnet to haul in and deport even those arrested for minor crimes. Enforcement advocates countered that to shield such people from deportation would be to encourage more illegal immigration.

Cecilia Munoz: From La Raza to the White House

President Obama's top adviser on immigration policy was Cecilia Munoz, the longtime vice-president and top lobbyist at the National Council of La Raza. Early in his first term, Obama named Munoz as the White House liaison with local and state governments. Newspaper profiles called Munoz, whose parents were immigrants from Bolivia, a "fierce" and even "ferocious" advocate of illegal immigrants.[178]

Munoz had a long record of opposing enforcement. Shortly after IRCA was passed, she called for repeal of employer sanctions. In the mid-1990s, she blasted the Jordan Commission's call for a computerized registry of authorized workers, calling it "worse than Big Brotherism" for Latinos.[179] Later she was active in the effort to block implementation of E-Verify, the computer-based system of worker verification. In 2000, the MacArthur Foundation awarded her a "genius" grant in recognition of her immigration advocacy. She also served on the boards of two foundations that donated millions of dollars to advocates for illegal immigrants, the Open Society Institute and the Atlantic Philanthropies.

One of Munoz's jobs at the White House was to defend Obama against the criticism of Latino activists who expected him to use his bully pulpit to press immediately for sweeping immigration reform. Meanwhile, enforcement advocates complained that the priority system was granting a de facto free pass to illegal immigrants who eluded the Border Patrol and used fraudulent documents to cheat the worksite verification system. They howled at an analogy that Cecilia Munoz used to defend Morton's prosecutorial discretion: "If you were running the police department of any urban area in this country, you would spend more resources going after serious criminals than after jaywalkers," said Munoz. "DHS is doing the immigration equivalent of the same thing." Fox News reported that story under the headline: "White House Compares Illegal Immigration to Jaywalking".[180]

Maria Hinojosa Comes Calling

When journalist Maria Hinojosa called on the White House as she worked on a 2011 "Frontline" documentary about the deportation controversy, Cecilia Munoz got the job of defending the administration. In an intense encounter with Hinojosa, who often straddled the line between reporting and advocacy, Munoz said the administration was obligated to carry out the deportation policies mandated by Congress.

"As long as Congress gives us the money to deport 400,000 people a year, that's what the administration is going to do," Munoz said. "That's our obligation under the law. We will be strategic about how we do it. ... But Congress passed a law, and Congress appropriates funds to implement that law, and the executive branch's job is to enforce it. How we do it matters a lot, but the president can't say to the Congress, 'I'm not going to bother to enforce this particular law because these are really compelling people.' That's not how democracy works."[181]

The interview was an excruciating task for Munoz. The "Frontline" documentary told stories of heartbreak for the children who stayed in the United States after their parents had been deported. The *Washington Post* reported that Munoz had been "targeted as a traitor by fellow Latinos in a highly personal, ethnic-based campaign against the president's deportation policies."[182] Hinojosa's brother, UCLA professor Raul Hinojosa, ratcheted up the pressure on the White House. He said activists believed that Obama was "prepared to sacrifice Latino families in a constant effort to placate the right" in pursuit of "an immigration reform negotiation that is not taking place."[183]

In early 2012, as President Obama neared the end of his first term, he appointed Munoz to the top White House job concerned with immigration. She became director of the Domestic Policy Council, which oversaw policy development for immigration and other issues such as education and health care. *Government Executive*, whose readership is primarily high-level employees of the federal government, reported that Munoz's appointment was a "signal to Hispanic voters that Obama has not given up on immigration reform, despite the lack of progress in his first term."[184]

Latino politicians and activists pressured Obama to assert executive authority to protect illegal immigrants from immigration enforcement. Obama, a former lecturer on constitutional law, demurred. "Now, I know some people want me to bypass Congress and change the laws on my own," he said. "And believe me, right now dealing with Congress. ... the idea of doing things on my own is very tempting. I promise you. Not just on immigration reform. But that's not how our system works."[185]

But in the summer of 2012, four months before a presidential election in which Obama was counting on Latino support, he changed course. Obama announced a program to suspend temporarily the threat of deportation and to grant work permits to the "Dreamers", the most sympathetic group of illegal immigrants, who had come to the United States as children. His executive order established a program called DACA (Deferred Action for Childhood Arrivals). He said congressional inaction had forced his hand.

Conservative critics accused Obama with taking a hammer to the constitutionally established separation of powers. Charles Krauthammer denounced the move as a "brazen end-run" around constitutional constraints and "the perfect pander" to Hispanic voters that would also have the effect of creating "a huge incentive for yet more illegal immigration."[186] He contrasted the president's action with his earlier resistance to demands that he act on his own. A year earlier Obama had said, "With respect to the notion that I can just suspend deportations through executive order, that's just not the case, because there are laws on the books that Congress has passed."

In the November election, Latinos gave 71 percent of their votes to Obama and just 27 percent to Republican Mitt Romney, who had favored constraints on illegal immigrants that would induce them to "self-deport". The Obama victory induced Republican Party leaders to make an assessment of the nation's immigration-driven demographic transformation. In their somber "autopsy" report, they concluded: "[W]e must embrace and champion comprehensive immigration reform. If we do not, our Party's appeal will continue to shrink to its core constituencies only."[187]

The Gang of Eight

In 2013, the bipartisan Gang of Eight senators — four Democrats and four Republicans — won Senate passage of a comprehensive reform bill. The measure was adopted by a wide margin despite warnings that it was once again fatally flawed by inadequate measures for worker verification. Then all eyes turned to the House, where Speaker John Boehner, fearing a fracture of his unruly caucus, refused to bring the bill up for a vote.

The following year, 2014, saw a steady escalation of tensions on both sides of the immigration divide. In March, Janet Murguia of NCLR, furious at the ongoing deportations, called Obama "the deporter-in-chief"[188] and demanded that he act unilaterally to protect millions more illegal immigrants. Obama, who wanted his presidency to be remembered as a parting of the waters for illegal immigrants, directed his legal advisers to draft a plan to do just that. The White House anticipated a roll-out before the November mid-term election.

Many Republicans were reluctant to resist the admonition of Gang of Eight member John McCain, who warned that failure to endorse the Senate-passed reform would be "catastrophic" for the GOP. "I have a tendency to agree with the head of the U.S. Chamber of Commerce, who said it doesn't matter who runs in 2016 if we don't do immigration reform," McCain said.[189]

Then came the fateful month of June. In Virginia's Seventh Congressional District, a little known college professor named David Brat, who made opposition to the comprehensive reform bill a centerpiece of his campaign, won a stunning Republican primary victory over House Majority leader Eric Cantor, who had tried to advance the reform. That seismic result sent shivers across the political landscape, including Democratic moderates who asked Obama to hold off any new executive action until after the November mid-term election. Another shock originated in the Rio Grande Valley of Texas, where tens of thousands of Central American children and then entire family units began pouring across the border and looking for the Border Patrol to take them in.

The stories of Central Americans streaming across the border intensified the immigration anxiety that had led to Cantor's defeat. The heightened sense of policy disorder and political risk intensified the anger of many Americans and destroyed the lingering hope for House passage of immigration reform.

In late November, after the mid-term elections, Obama issued another executive order that delighted advocates of unauthorized immigrants. He established a program that would be known as DAPA — Deferred Action for Parents of Americans and Lawful Permanent Residents. It was intended to shield several million more people from enforcement of federal immigration law. Obama pitched it as a measure to target deportations at "felons, not families". DAPA, however, was halted by a federal judge in a 2015 decision that was upheld a year later by a deadlocked Supreme Court.

A Tale of Two Senators: Schumer and Portman

Barely noticed within the immigration Sturm und Drang at the White House, a drama unfolded in the Senate Chamber in 2013 that in the long run may be more important to the effort to repair the nation's broken immigration system. It was a struggle over proposals in the Gang of Eight bill to replace the much-maligned I-9 worker verification process, which remained in place despite decades of reports about its inadequacies and pleas for Congress to replace it with a system not so vulnerable to fraud.

The drama was a battle of wills between two emblematic figures in the immigration debate, a Democrat and a Republican, whose approaches were shaped by their contrasting personalities, sensibilities, and conceptions of the challenge of reforming immigration law, especially at the worksite.

The Democrat was Chuck Schumer, a liberal from New York. He is a brash, impatient man of perpetual motion, who relishes being in the thick of the action and at the center of attention. He is driven by a will to cut deals, stroke egos, forge alliances, and build consensus to get bills passed. "I love to legislate," Schumer said in 1998, during his first campaign for the Senate. He described that art this way: "Taking an idea — often not original with me — shaping it, molding it, building a coalition of people who might not completely agree with it."[190]

Schumer is a compulsive deal-maker. His urge to reconcile opposite sides of an issue seems to be an extension of his knack for brokering romances within his staff. The *New York Times*, describing Schumer's inclination to "cajole, nag, and outright pester his staff ... toward connubial bliss", called him "the Yenta of the Senate".[191]

Schumer was a key broker of the Immigration Reform and Control Act of 1986. The *Houston Chronicle* reported then that he "was so determined to forge enough compromises to pass the bill that some lobbyists dubbed him 'The Monty Hall of Immigration.'"[192] That was a reference to the host of the frenetic television game show "Let's Make a Deal". Schumer cut the deal to placate California agribusiness by offering amnesty not just to illegal immigrants who had been in the country for five years, but also to farm workers who had picked crops for a mere 90 days. That Special Agricultural Worker amnesty, as we have seen, would be swamped by fraud.

Rob Portman is an establishment Republican from Ohio. He operates in a lower key. He is as understated as Schumer is brash, as polished as Schumer is rumpled. He has the physical confidence of an outdoorsman who has kayaked the length of the Rio Grande and who once worked on a Texas cattle ranch. Despite those interests, the Capitol Hill newspaper *Roll Call* pointed to Portman's "Midwestern wonk character" as "part of his appeal". It described him as "most comfortable rattling off statistics about the deficit".[193] His credentials as former head of the Office of Management and Budget and chief U.S. trade representative are part of a packed resume that made him a finalist to be Mitt Romney's vice presidential running mate.

Portman immersed himself in immigration policy in the late 1970s as a staffer on the Select Commission on Immigration and Refugee Policy. Chaired by the Rev. Theodore Hesburgh, president of Notre Dame, SCIRP comprised 16 members — four from the Senate, four from the House, four cabinet members, and four members of the public. Its final report, issued in 1981, laid the policy foundations on which IRCA was passed five years later.

If Schumer can be seen as the id of immigration policymaking — eager and insistent — Portman is the superego, assessing risks and warning of consequences. If Schumer is its broker, Portman is its quality control engineer. If what Schumer fears most is failure to produce a bill, Portman warns about the futility of passing a defective bill that is bound to fail. Schumer was the irrepressible driving force within the bipartisan Gang of Eight, a group whose efforts Portman viewed with a mixture of admiration and skepticism.

Portman supported the Gang of Eight bill's provisions to address the concerns of important groups, especially the advocates of illegal immigrants who would be put on a path to citizenship and the employers who would be given access to hundreds of thousands of additional immigrant workers. But he believed that the bill, far from solving the problem of worker verification, would compound it, extending the past failures far into the future. Rather than showing Congress's ability to solve problems, he believed, it would demonstrate its capacity to perpetuate them. He was convinced that the promised reform would prove to be another damaging policy failure.

Portman was haunted by IRCA's failure. He saw it as corrosive not only of immigration control but also of public trust in government. "The 1986 bill casts a long shadow on this place," Portman said in his June 26 exchange with Schumer, "and we've got to be sure we don't repeat those mistakes."

During the long debate that preceded its passage, as the Senate moved toward its vote on the Gang of Eight bill in late June, Portman joined Montana Democrat Jon Tester in offering an amendment that aimed to strengthen E-Verify, an Internet-based program that allows employers to check whether a new hire is authorized to work. They believed that the version of E-Verify included in the Senate bill was vulnerable to fraud. Their warning echoed a concern voiced by the *New York Times* back in 1980, when the House of Representatives was in the early stages of a debate that led to IRCA: "Without effective verification, there can be no effective enforcement of the borders," said a *Times* editorial. "Without effective enforcement, there can be no immigration reform worthy of the name. The choice for the House is clear: legislate or pretend."[194]

Portman believed that the Senate bill was a form of pretending. He thought worker verification had been compromised to placate powerful political and economic interests, just as it had been in 1986. "Look, it is, frankly, not a very popular part of the legislation, and over the years it hasn't been," Portman said. "In 1986 it wasn't. That is why it was never implemented, because there is sort of an unholy alliance among employers, among those representing labor union members, among those representing certain constituent groups who feel there might be some discrimination or other issues."

100

Portman insisted that the Senate take a firm stand: "We believe — and I am passionate about this, as you can tell — that if we don't fix the workplace, we cannot have an immigration system that works," he said.

As detailed in his amendment, Portman wanted to expedite the rollout of E-Verify, putting it on a more rapid timetable for large employers than called for in the Senate bill. To improve the accuracy of E-Verify and reduce identity fraud, he wanted to strengthen the photo-matching process known as Photo Tool, which would enable employers to match a photo ID provided by the employee with a digital photo stored in an E-Verify database. Portman wanted to double the federal grant money to states that make their driver's license photos available to E-Verify. He proposed to address privacy concerns by prohibiting the use of those shared photos for anything other than E-Verify.

Portman and Tester wanted Senate Majority Leader Harry Reid (D-Nev.) to allow a brief floor discussion of their amendment and a separate vote. Portman explained his frustration with Reid's refusal. "To not have a separate debate and a separate vote on this amendment, on this issue," he said, "does not give us the possibility of sending this over to the House with a strong message and maximizing the chance the House of Representatives will see that strong bipartisan vote on this important issue of workplace enforcement. ... It is that simple."

Schumer, ironically, said he supported the upgraded E-Verify in the Portman-Tester amendment. But he was trying to guide the bill past a quarrel between Reid and Chuck Grassley over how many amendments would be brought to the floor before the final vote. For Schumer, the Portman amendment had become a nuisance, an obstacle in the way of an historic bill that would bring legalization for millions and provide employers access to hundreds of thousands of additional foreign workers every year. With his eyes on that big prize, Schumer was irritated by Portman's fixation on technical detail.

Schumer used multiple tactics on the Senate floor, soothing Portman and then cajoling him. Harry Reid mocked Portman's refusal to have the amendment subsumed into the several hundred pages of an amendment that Schumer had just brokered with Sens. Bob Corker (R-Tenn.) and John Hoeven (R-N.D.).

That amendment sought to win Republican votes by doubling the Border Patrol and spending an astonishing $42 billion on border security. Such extravagance made sense only as a ploy to win a few Republican votes. It had little chance of surviving the legislative gauntlet. But Reid, irritated at Portman's stubbornness, accused the Ohioan of theatrics, complaining, "He wants a big show out here to have a separate vote."

Portman conceded Reid's point. Normally un-theatrical, Portman believed that the debate was necessary. Given the long history of failed enforcement, he believed the debate would help build a record of firm congressional intent. He believed it would allow Congress to make a statement of atonement for the sins of IRCA. It would be a statement that this time Congress was serious, that it would not accept a failure like the one that had followed IRCA, that it would insist on developing, funding, implementing, and enforcing a system that would deliver what Congress promised.

Schumer was the expansively reformist liberal. He was determined to take bold action, confident in his good intentions, and eager to pass a bill. Portman was the cautiously reformist conservative, He was wary of promises that would exceed the grasp of legislation and thereby aggravate the problem it sought to control.

The contrasting priorities of these two lawmakers will almost certainly re-emerge in any future congressional discussion of immigration reform. The challenge for those who seek reform will be to enact legislation that incorporates necessary compromises and trade-offs without crippling enforcement within the interior of the United States.

Afterword:
The Trump Administration

Alarm at illegal immigration was one of the principal themes of the presidential campaign of Donald Trump, whose pledges to stop it conveyed his challenge to Republican elites and endeared him to many working class Americans. Even critics who were appalled at the prospect of a Trump presidency acknowledged that he had illuminated a crisis that many failed to understand. "People across America have been falling through the cracks," wrote *New York Times* columnist David Brooks. "Trump to his credit made them visible."

Trump's aggressive stand against illegal immigration included denunciation of Mexican migrants as criminals and rapists, a vow to build a border wall and send the bill to Mexico, and condemnation of rivals such as Florida Senator Marco Rubio for helping to win Senate passage of the comprehensive immigration reform bill that later withered in the House of Representatives. Early in 2016, Trump pledged to unwind executive orders issued by President Obama to provide legal status to "Dreamers" and other illegal immigrants. "After my inauguration, for the first time in decades, Americans will wake up in a country where their immigration laws are enforced," he promised.

Trump repeatedly declared his allegiance to Americans who had been battered by the forces of globalization, illegal immigration, and failed enforcement of IRCA. "We need a system that serves our needs, not the needs of others," he said. "Remember: under a Trump administration it's called America first." But after Trump's populist nationalism had carried him to the presidency, the contrast between two of his cabinet picks highlighted the difficulty of finding a coherent and consistent approach to illegal immigration, especially at the worksite.

On the one hand, Trump's nominee to be attorney general, Sen. Jeff Sessions, was a prominent anti-illegal immigration hawk. But his first choice to be labor secretary, Andrew Puzder, was an executive in the fast-food franchising industry, which had a troubled history of worksite enforcement violations. Puzder eventually withdrew from consideration after a storm of protest against his generally laissez faire attitude about immigration.

A centerpiece of the Trump presidential campaign was a more robust E-Verify program. The campaign website, promising "Immigration Reform That Will Make America Great Again", called for making E-Verify mandatory and asserted that "this simple measure will protect jobs for unemployed Americans." Trump had also vowed to "fight to make American workers safer and more prosperous" by providing "more jobs and better wages for the American worker."

Trump has equivocated on the prospects for comprehensive reform legislation. He initially denounced proposals for legalization of illegal immigrants, but later indicated that he would be open to legalization under certain circumstances. He has sometimes vacillated within the space of a few seconds. For example, in his visit to Arizona before the election, Trump at first took the hard-line stance that "you cannot obtain legal status or become a citizen of the United States by illegally entering the country." But then he went on to make this qualified and cryptic offer: "Importantly, in several years when we have accomplished all of our enforcement and deportation goals and truly ended illegal immigration for good, including the construction of a great wall, which we will have built in record time and at a reasonable cost — which you never hear from the government — and establishment of our new lawful immigration system. Then and only then will we be in a position to consider the appropriate disposition of those individuals who remain."

106

It remains to be seen how the Trump administration will proceed with the two basic approaches to worksite enforcement: the raids aimed at arresting illegal workers and the audits that target scofflaw employers. Trump's campaign centerpiece, a big, beautiful border wall that Mexico would pay for, has run into a congressional wall of its own and a furious nationalistic response in Mexico. Retired ICE special agent Claude Arnold said that while a border wall makes enforcement sense in some areas, "If you don't address the employment magnet and hold employers accountable, you're not going to be effective in curbing illegal immigration."

End Notes

[1] President Reagan's signing statement, November 6, 1986.

[2] Office of the Inspector General, Department of Justice.

[3] "U.S. Immigration Policy and the National Interest", Select Commission on Immigration and Refugee Policy, March 1981, p. 60.

[4] House Judiciary Committee, 1086, "Immigration Control and Legalization Amendments Act of 1986," Report 99-682, Part 1. Washington, D.C.; U.S. Government Printing Office.

[5] David A. Martin, "Eight Myths About Immigration Enforcement", *New York University Journal of Legislation and Public Policy*, 10 (2006-2007): 525, 544.

[6] Katherine McIntire Peters," "A House Divided", *Government Executive* magazine, November 1, 1998.

[7] Author interview with retired INS agent.

[8] Author interview with Susan Martin, January 8, 2016.

[9] Patrick Buchanan, *The Great Betrayal: How American Sovereignty and Social Justice Are Being Sacrificed to the Gods of the Global Economy*, Boston: Little, Brown, 1998.

[10] INS Commissioner Alan Nelson, press conference, October 8, 1987.

[11] Author interview with Schroeder.

[12] Zita Arocha, "INS tries a new approach", *The Washington Post*, August 23, 1987.

[13] Mary Ann Galante, "Sting of New Immigration Law Felt in a Labor-Short County: Hotels/Owners Could Be Forced to Lure Workers With Higher Wages", *Los Angeles Times*, October 18, 1987.

[14] Eric Schine, "Sanctions Fail to Cut Alien Jobs; Threat of Penalties Ignored in Hiring of Illegal Workers", *Los Angeles Times,* May 2, 1988.

[15] Michael Bigelow, "The Immigration Dilemma: Survey Raises Doubts About U.S. Law's Effectiveness", *San Francisco Chronicle*, July 5, 1989.

[16] *1990 Statistical Yearbook of the Immigration and Naturalization Service, 1990,* Immigration and Naturalization Service, December 1991, p. 163.

[17] Julie Brossy, "Aliens Entering Without Papers Show Sharp Rise", *San Diego Tribune*, March 12, 1990.

[18] Robert Bach and Doris Meissner, "Employment and Immigration Reform: Employer Sanctions Four Years Later." p. 298, *The Paper Curtain*, Michael Fix ed., Washington: The Urban Institute Press, 1991.

[19] Interview with author, December 2016.

[20] Michael Fix and Paul Hill, "Implementing Sanctions: Reports from the Field," in *The Paper Curtain, op, cit.* p. 78.

[21] Kim I. Mills "Immigration Law Poorly Enforced, Congressman Says", Associated Press, March 21, 1989.

[22] Author interview with Shaw, February 2017.

[23] Roberto Suro, "Migrants' False Claims: Fraud on a Huge Scale", *The New York Times,* November 12, 1989.

[24] Eric Schlosser, "In the Strawberry Fields", *The Atlantic*, November 1995.

[25] Philip Martin, "Hired Farm Workers", *Choices: The Magazine of Food, Farm, and Resource Issues*, Vol. 27, No 2, 2nd Quarter 2012.

[26] Author interview with Shaw, February 2017.

[27] Author interview with Lucero, January 2017.

[28] Author interview with Moon, October, 2016.

[29] Dan Cadman, "Lessons Learned by an Insider in the 30 Years Since IRCA", Center for Immigration Studies blog post, October 26, 2016.

[30] Author interview with Yates, January 2017.

[31] John M. Crewdson, "U.S. Immigration Service Hampered by Corruption", *The New York Times*, January 13, 1980.

[32] Email from McGraw to author, February 2, 2017.

[33] *Collins Foods International, Inc., Petitioner, v. U.S. Immigration and Naturalization Service, Respondent*, 948 F.2d 549 (9th Cir. 1991).

[34] "Illegal Aliens: Significant Obstacles to Reducing Unauthorized Alien Employment Exist", U.S. General Accounting Office, April 1999.

[35] Demetrios A. Papademetriou, B. Lindsay Lowell, and Deborah A. Cobb-Clark, "Employer Sanctions: Expectations and Early Outcomes", *The Paper Curtain, op. cit.*, p 228.

[36] Michael Fix, at news conference sponsored by the Urban Institute and the Rand Corporation, March 15, 1990.

[37] Dan Freedman, "Lack of Standardization Blamed for INS Inequities", *San Antonio Light*, March 25, 1991.

[38] *Ibid.*

[39] Bill McAllister, "Parting Shots at 'Totally Disorganized' INS", *The Washington Post*, October 18, 1989.

[40] Pamela J. Podger, "Border Patrol to Quit Valley?" *Fresno Bee*, July 15, 1991.

[41] Author interview with Bednarz, March 2017.

[42] "Immigration Reform: Employer Sanctions and the Question of Discrimination", General Accounting Office, March 1990.

[43] Senate Judiciary Committee hearing, "The GAO Report on Employer Sanctions and Discrimination," March 20 and April 20, 1990; transcript, video.

[44] *Ibid.*

[45] Yzaguirre quoted in Bach and Meissner, chapter in *The Paper Chase, op. cit.*, p. 289

[46] Cecilia Munoz, "Unfinished Business: The Immigration Reform and Control Act of 1986", Policy Analysis Center, Office of Research, Advocacy and Legislation of the National Council of La Raza, 1990, p. 54.

[47] Associated Press, "Deportation 'Flaw'Assailed", *St. Louis Post Dispatch*, April 16, 1990; and Charlotte Grimes, "McNary Is Challenged on Illegal Immigrants", *St Louis Post Dispatch*, April 21, 1990.

[48] Justin Wm. Moyer, "The forgotten story of how refugees almost ended Bill Clinton's Career", *The Washington Post*, November 17, 2015.

[49] Tim Weiner, "Pleas for Asylum Inundate System for Immigration", *The New York Times*, April 25, 1993.

[50] Hearing of the Subcommittee on Immigration and Claims of the House Judiciary Committee, "Immigration and Naturalization Service's Interior Enforcement Strategy", July 1, 1999, p. 108.

[51] William Branigin, "Immigration Fraud Schemes Proliferating Inside U.S.", *The Washington Post*, May 19, 1997.

[52] Roberto Suro, "California Border Crackdown Vowed; With the Administration Under Fire, Reno Promises a New Effort", *The Washington Post*, September 18, 1994.

[53] Jeffrey Passel, "U.S. Immigration: Numbers, Trends, and Outlook", Pew Hispanic Center, March 26, 2007, pp. 12-13.

[54] Laura Mecoy, "Despite 187, Fake ID Sales Booming: Proposition Has Done Little to Slow Flow of Counterfeit Documents", *Sacramento Bee*, December 12, 1994.

[55] Paul Feldman, "INS Breaks Up Ring that Makes Fake I.D.s", *Los Angeles Times*, January 4, 1995.

[56] Philip Martin, "INS Evaluates Gatekeeper, SouthPAW", *Migration News*, October 1995, Volume 2, Number 10.

[57] "U.S. Immigration Policy: Restoring Credibility", U.S. Commission on Immigration Reform, September 1994, p. 14.

[58] William Douglas, "Panel: Check Immigrants at Jobs", *Newsday*, August 4, 1994.

[59] Marcus Stern, "Illegal Immigration Bill Weakened by Unlikely Alliance", Copley News Service, November 4, 1995.

[60] Paolo Pereznieto, "The Case of Mexico's 1995 Peso Crisis And Argentina's 2002 Convertibility Crisis", UNICEF, December 2010.

[61] Gilbert Klein, "Cost of illegal immigration is high", *Richmond Times-Dispatch*, April 17, 1994.

[62] Feinstein statement on the Senate floor, May 1, 1996.

[63] Mary Beth Rogers, *Barbara Jordan: An American Hero*, New York: Bantam Books, 1998, p. 325.

[64] Gustavo Lopez and Kristen Bialik, "Key Findings About U.S. Immigrants", Pew Research Center, May 3, 2017.

[65] Patrick J. McDonnell, "INS to Get Tough With Employers", *Los Angeles Times*, May 7, 1995.

[66] Author interview with Bargerhuff, March 2017.

[67] Author interview with Fischer, February 2017.

[68] INS Internal document, "PROPOSED OPERATION SOUTHPAW PHASE II," provided by confidential source who participated in the operation.

[69] "Worksite Enforcement: Reducing the Job Magnet", Immigration and Naturalization Service, June 1996.

[70] Video of INS raid in Dalton, Georgia, available at U.S. Citizenship & Immigration Services History Library, Washington, D.C.

[71] Sandra Sanchez, "Heat Being Turned Up on Illegal Immigrants: Some Believe Politics Behind Increased Raids", *USA Today*, September 29, 1995.

[72] Interview with Fischer, *op. cit.*

[73] Jordan testimony before the U.S. Senate Committee on the Judiciary Subcommittee on Immigration and Refugee Affairs, August, 3, 1994.

[74] Robert Pear, "Clinton Embraces a Proposal to Cut Immigration by a Third", *The New York Times*, June 8, 1995.

[75] Conyers, Congressional Record, March 20, 1996, pH2497.

[76] Frank, Congressional Record, March 20, 1996, pH2498.

[77] "Immigration and Naturalization Service Oversight", Senate Judiciary Subcommittee on Immigration, October 2, 1996, p. 40.

[78] *Ibid.*, p. 32.

[79] *Ibid.*

[80] Micah Bump, Andy Schoenholtz, Susan Martin, and B. Lindsay Lowell, "Controlling Irregular Immigration: The Challenge of Worksite Enforcement", Institute for the Study of International Migration, September 2007.

[81] Michael Kranish, "Clinton Policy Shift Followed Asian-American Fund-Raiser", *Boston Globe*, January 16, 1997.

[82] Richard T. Cooper, "How DNC Got Caught in a Donor Dilemma", *Los Angeles Times*, December 23, 1996.

[83] Edward Walsh and Lena H. Sun, "Panel Examines Hiring of Huang at Commerce", *The Washington Post*, July 17, 1997.

[84] Meissner press briefing, October 29, 1996.

[85] William J. Clinton, "Statement on the Executive Order on Illegal Immigration", February 13, 1996.

[86] Kevin Johnson "Deportation of illegals is up 62% over 1996", *USA Today*, October 31, 1997.

[87] Jules Witcover, "Dole Launches Ariz. Campaign in Buchanan's Wake", *Baltimore Sun*, February 25, 1996.

[88] Gregory R. Jones "INS Raids", *Macon Telegraph*, May 14, 1998.

[89] Marcus Stern, "A Semi-Tough Policy on Illegal Workers" *The Washington Post*, July 5, 1998.

[90] Author interview with Szafnicki, November 2016.

[91] Martin, "Eight Myths About Immigration Enforcement," *op. cit.*

[92] Author interview with Martin, February 2017.

[93] 1996 Senate Judiciary Immigration Subcommittee hearing, *op. cit.* p 6.

[94] *Ibid.*, p. 9.

[95] DOJ Office of the Inspector General, "Inspections Report".

[96] Paul Hutchinson, "INS raid reveals labor woes U.S. workers don't want low-paying jobs", *Denver Post*, March 23, 1997.

[97] *Ibid.*

[98] Lars-Erik Nelson, "Congress Won't risk Alienating Big Business", *New York Daily News*, September 30, 1996.

[99] Chishti at hearing of the House Judiciary Subcommittee on Immigration and Claims, "Immigration and Naturalization Service's Interior Enforcement Strategy", July 1, 1999, p. 209.

[100] Senate Judiciary Immigration Subcommittee, oversight hearing, October 2, 1996, *op. cit.*, p. 26.

[101] Jerry Kammer "Illegals on Job Being Ignored: Border Patrol Build-up No Help at Work Sites", *Arizona Republic*, November 30, 1998.

[102] Quoted by Sen. Alan Simpson in his opening statement of a Senate Judiciary Committee immigration subcommittee hearing on October 2, 1996, *op. cit.* p. 2.

[103] Statement of GAO Director of Homeland Security and Justice Division Richard Stana at the hearing of the Subcommittee on Immigration and Claims of the House Judiciary Committee, "Immigration and Naturalization Service's Interior Enforcement Strategy", July 1, 1999, p. 50.

[104] "INS: Fewer Workplace Raids," *Migration News*, April 1999.

[105] Ana Aca, Diego Bunuel, and Maria A. Morales, "Brutal INS Raid Angers Public; Justice Department Set to Investigate", *Miami Herald*, April 25, 1998.

[106] Luisa Yanez, "INS Raids Flower Company. Congressman Asks Reno to Investigate 'Thug-Like' Operation", *South Florida Sun-Sentinel*, April 26, 1998.

[107] Ana Aca, Diego Bunuel, and Maria A. Morales, *op.cit.*

[108] "Fiscal Year 1998 Fourth Quarter Performance Review, Interior Enforcement", internal INS document, December 18, 1998.

[109] Robert Bach, "Mexican Immigration and the American State", *International Migration Review*, Vol. 12, No. 4, Special Issue: (Winter 1978), pp. 536-558.

[110] Bach and Meissner, "Employment and Immigration Reform: Employer Sanctions Four Years Later", *The Paper Curtain*, *op. cit.*, pp. 281-302.

[111] House Judiciary Subcommittee on Immigration and Claims, "Designations of Temporary Protected Status and Fraud in Prior Amnesty Programs", March 4, 1999, pp 57-63.

[112] Ned Glascock and Craig Whitlock, "Law vs. Reality", *News and Observer*, November 30, 1998. (In the interest of clarity and context, this excerpt is more complete than the one inserted into the hearing record.)

[113] Interview with Bednarz, March 2017.

[114] Kevin Phillips, *Arrogant Capital: Washington, Wall Street, and the Frustration of American Politics*, Boston: Little, Brown; 1994, p. xv.

[115] Robert J. Samuelson, "Build a Fence — and Amnesty", *The Washington Post*, March 8, 2006.

[116] Michael Hedges, Scripps Howard News Service, "Chasing Immigrants No Long Priority. Agency's New Policy On Illegal Residents Raises Concerns in Congress", *Milwaukee Journal Sentinel*, March 6, 1999.

[117] Bach and Meissner, *op. cit.*, p. 298.

[118] William Branigin, "INS Shifts 'Interior' Strategy to Target Criminal Aliens", *The Washington Post*, March 15, 1999.

[119] House Subcommittee on Immigration and Claims, "Immigration and Naturalization Service's Interior Enforcement Strategy", July 1, 1999, p. 9.

[120] *Ibid.*, p. 31.

[121] Laurie P. Cohen, "Meatpacker Taps Mexican Labor Force, Thanks to Help from INS Program", *Wall Street Journal*, October 15, 1998.

[122] Hammond testimony at a hearing of the House Subcommittee on Immigration and Claims, "Immigration and Naturalization Service's Interior Enforcement Strategy," July 1, 1999, p. 134.

[123] *Ibid.*, p 119.

[124] Eric Schlosser, *Fast Food Nation,* Boston: Houghton Mifflin, 2001.

[125] "Operation Vanguard, IBP", Rural Migration News, Volume 5, Number 3, July 1999.

[126] Leslie Reed, "Task Force Rips Vanguard Recommendations Include Amnesty for Immigrant Workers", *Omaha World Herald*, October 16, 2000.

[127] "2000 Statistical Yearbook of the Immigration and Naturalization Service", September 2002, Table 60.

[128] Meissner on C-SPAN's "Washington Journal", March 29, 2007.

[129] Hearing of the Senate Subcommittee on Immigration and Refugee Policy, "The Knowing Employment of Illegal Immigrants," September 30, 1981, p. 5.

[130] *Ibid.*, p. 194.

[131] Nancy Cleeland, "Unionizing Is Catch-22 for Illegal Immigrants", *Los Angeles Times*, January 16, 2000.

[132] Frank Swoboda, "Unions Reverse on Illegal Aliens", *The Washington Post,* February 17, 2000.

[133] Louis Uchitelle, "I.N.S. Is Looking the Other Way As Illegal Immigrants Fill Jobs", *The New York Times*, March 9, 2000.

[134] "The Immigration Debate in 2000", National Immigration Forum panel, February 23, 2000.

[135] Alex Aleinikoff, "Illegal Employers", *American Prospect*, December 4, 2000.

[136] James Goldsborough, "Out of Control Immigration", *Foreign Affairs,* September/October 2000.

[137] Jared Bernstein, *Crunch: Why Do I Feel So Squeezed? (And Other Unsolved Economic Mysteries)*, Oakland, Calif.: Berrett-Koehler Publishers, 2008, p. 157.

[138] Carla Marinucci, "Reaching Out to State's Latinos, Bush Distances Himself From Pete Wilson", *Houston Chronicle,* April 8, 2000.

[139] "Republican Party Platform of 1996", August 12, 1996.

[140] "A weak choice. INS needs more than a political appointee", *San Diego Union Tribune,* May 1, 2001.

[141] Thomas R. Eldridge, Susan Ginsburg, Walter T. Hempel II, Janice L. Kephart, and Kelly Moore "9/11 and Terrorist Travel, A Staff Report of the National Commission on Terrorist Attacks Upon the United States", August 21, 2004, p. 110.

[142] *Ibid.*, p. 101.

[143] Belinda I. Reyes, Hans P. Johnson, Richard Van Swearingen, "Holding the Line? The Effect of the Recent Border Build-up on Unauthorized Immigration", Public Policy Institute of California, 2002.

[144] Philip Wrona, "U.S. Immigration and Customs Enforcement: Dysfunctional Not by Design", Naval Post Graduate School thesis, March 2007.

[145] Alison Siskin, Andorra Bruno, Blas Nunez-Neto, Lisa M. Seghetti, and Ruth Ellen Wasem, "Immigration Enforcement Within the United States", Congressional Research Service, August 6, 2006, p. 40.

146 "Report to Congressional Requesters: Immigration Enforcement: Weaknesses Hinder Employment Verification and Worksite Enforcement Efforts", Government Accountability Office, August 2005, p, 32.

147 Statement of Richard M. Stana, director, justice issues, "Immigration Enforcement: Challenges to Implementing the INS Interior Enforcement Strategy", General Accounting Office press release, June 19, 2002, p. 3.

148 "Washington/Baltimore High Intensity Drug Trafficking Area Drug Market Analysis", National Drug Intelligence Center, June 2007.

149 Stephanie Hanes, "More than 24 foreign nationals with sex offense records arrested Actions in Md. are part of nationwide crackdown", *Baltimore Sun*, August 19, 2004.

150 "Immigration Enforcement Within the United States", *op. cit.*, p. 41, Table 1.

151 Laura Frank, "Crackdown on illegals: 38 Commerce City workers arrested, part of national investigation", *Rocky Mountain News*, April 21, 2006; see also "IFCO Systems Managers Charged with Unlawful Employment of Illegal Aliens", Department of Justice press release, June 2, 2010.

152 Jerry Kammer, "The 2006 Swift Raids: Assessing the Impact of Immigration Enforcement Actions at Six Facilities", Center for Immigration Studies, March 18, 2009.

153 CQ Transcripts Wire, "President Bush Addresses U.S. Chamber of Commerce on Immigration", *The Washington Post*, June 1, 2006.

154 Spencer S. Hsu and Kari Lyderson, "Illegal Hiring is Rarely Penalized," *Washington Post,* June 19, 2006.

155 Silvestre Reyes on C-SPAN's "Washington Journal", August 17, 2006.

156 Karen Lee Ziner, "Bianco workers allege violations", *Providence Journal,* March 20, 2007; see also "Fines issued for New Bedford factory targeted in immigration raid", Associated Press, July 6, 2007; see also: "Raid shows need for immigration policy," editorial, *The Washington Post* editorial, March 20, 2007.

[157] Sen. Kennedy press release, "New Bedford Immigration Raid Devastation Reminiscent of Hurricane Katrina", US Federal News, March 13, 2007.

[158] Carol Rose and Christopher Ott, "Immigration raid was just one of many", *Boston Globe*, March 26, 2007.

[159] Jerry Seper, "Chertoff defends ICE raid on illegals. Rejects complaint from Kennedy", *Washington Times*, March 22, 2007.

[160] Hearing of the Senate Subcommittee on Immigration, Border Security, and Citizenship, "Immigration Enforcement at the Workplace: Learning From the Mistakes of 1986", June 19, 2006.

[161] "The 1986 Immigration Law", "Washington Journal", C-SPAN, May 29, 2007.

[162] Author interview with Baker, November 2016.

[163] Gladwin Hill, "3 U.S. Officials Accuse Farmers of Forcing Illicit Mexican Labor", *The New York Times*, August 9, 1951.

[164] Robert L. Bach, *Latin Journey: Cuban and Mexican Immigrants in the United States*," Berkeley, University of California Press, 1985, p. 14-15.

[165] Stana testimony at hearing of House Homeland Security Subcommittee on Border and Maritime Security, "A Study in Contrasts: House and Senate Approaches to Border Security", July 23, 2013.

[166] Barack Obama, *The Audacity of Hope: Thoughts on Reclaiming the American Dream*, 2006, New York: Three Rivers Press, p. 260.

[167] *Ibid.,* p. 263.

[168] "Obama Addresses the National Council of La Raza", transcript, *The Washington Post*, July 15, 2008.

[169] Stephen Dinan, "Illegals Raid Dismays Obama Voters", *Washington Times*, February 26, 2009.

[170] Elise Fialkowski, Kate Kalmykov, "Immigration compliance vital to avoid fines, criminal sanctions", *Nation's Restaurant News*, December 14, 2009.

[171] Figures provided by by ICE Western Region Communications Office.

[172] Statement of Laurie E. Ekstrand, GAO, before the House Subcommittee on International Law, Immigration and Refugees, September 21, 1994.

[173] Erin Kelly, "U.S. to Expand Workplace Immigration Audits", Gannett News Service, November 19, 2009.

[174] Lamar Smith, Hearing of the House Subcommittee on Immigration and Border Security, "E-Verify Program Benefits", February 27, 2013.

[175] Morton on C-SPAN's "Washington Journal", August 8, 2010.

[176] Brendan Sasso, "Obama: Deportation Statistics 'deceptive'", *The Hill*, September 28, 2011.

[177] DHS Office of Inspector General, "Immigration and Custom Enforcement Detention Bed space Management", April 2009.

[178] Peter Wallsten, "From fierce activist to White House defender", *The Washington Post*, November 10, 2011; see also, David Nakamura, "White House immigration adviser Cecilia Munoz is taking the heat for Obama", *The Washington Post,* September 8, 2014.

[179] William Douglas, "Panel: Check Immigrants at Jobs", *Newsday*, August 4, 1994.

[180] Edwin Mora, "White House Compares Illegal Immigration to Jaywalking", Fox News, September 14, 2011.

[181] Transcript of "Lost in Detention", "Frontline", October 18, 2011.

[182] Peter Wallsten, "From fierce activist to White House defender", *The Washington Post,* November 10, 2011.

[183] Univision newscast, April 12, 2011; see also Jerry Kammer, "Univision Does It Again", Center for Immigration Studies blog, April 13, 2011.

[184] Andrew Joseph, "Immigration-reform advocate to lead Domestic Policy Council", *Government Executive*, January 10, 2012.

[185] "Remarks by the President on Comprehensive Immigration Reform in El Paso, Texas", States News Service, May 10, 2011.

[186] Charles Krauthammer, "Obama's amnesty-by-fiat—naked lawlessness", *The Washington Post*, June 21, 2012.

[187] Chris Cillizza, "Three sentences on immigration that will haunt Republicans in 2016", *The Washington Post*, July 1, 2014.

[188] "Latino leader calls Obama 'deporter-in-chief'", EFE World News Service, March 5, 2014.

[189] Dan Nowicki, "Little Hope Remains for Reform One Year After 'Gang of 8' Bill", *Arizona Republic*, June 25, 2014.

[190] Adam Nagourney, "Upbeat Schumer Battles Poor Polls, Low Turnouts and His Image", *The New York Times*, May 16, 1998.

[191] Michael Grynbaum, "Senator, Senator, Make Me a Match: For Staff, Schumer Is Cupid", *The New York Times*, August 17, 2012.

[192] Judy Wiessler, "Immigration Bill: déjà vu, yet different", *Houston Chronicle*, October 12, 1986.

[193] Meredith Shiner, "Portman Quietly Positions Himself, but for What", *Roll Call*, March 11, 2013.

[194] "Guerrilla War on Immigration", *The New York Times*, August 27, 1982.

Made in the USA
Middletown, DE
20 September 2017